MY LIFE WITH THE STARS
- sizzling secrets spilled!
(SECOND EDITION)

Tony Flood

MY LIFE WITH THE STARS
SECOND EDITION

Published in the UK in August, 2019 by Antony Flood and SW Communications. The original edition was published in the UK in April, 2012 by MyVoice Publishing.

DEDICATIONS

This book is dedicated to the memory of my parents Mabel and Dennis Flood and my wonderful grandparents Winnie and Reggie Burwash, who brought me up with love and kindness.

They, together with my lovely wife Heather and also much loved son James, have played vital parts in my life, as have other relatives and friends. It was Heather who suggested I write 'My Life With The Stars'.

I am grateful for the supportive endorsements provided for this book by comedians Al Murray and Tim Vine, boxing legend Frank Bruno, singers Anita Harris and Dec Cluskey, of The Bachelors, actresses Shirley Anne Field, Susie Amy and the late June Whitfield, actors Brian Capron, Daniel Hill and Denis Lill, soccer icon Malcolm Macdonald, former Manchester United manager Tommy Docherty and Daily Mail sports writer Sami Mokbel.

Thanks, too, to Dave Davies for supplying the picture of his client Frank Bruno, and to David Allen of Allen David International Entertainments, Dave Smith, Ted Cassell, Peter Turner, Barry King, Mark Dimmock, Jeff Klepper, Graham Dunn, Jeff Morton, Brian Francis, Tricia Sneath and others for providing pictures.

Special thanks go to my previous publishers Rupert Barlow and Rex Sumner, marketing experts PublishingPush and to Diny van Kleeff, who has formatted this new edition.

PRAISE FOR MY LIFE WITH THE STARS

The Pub Landlord AL MURRAY says: "A book that calls me one of Britain's great comedians has got to be worth reading! Tony Flood's My Life With The Stars is full of amusing anecdotes and sizzling secrets about BIG names from showbiz and sport."

Singer and actress ANITA HARRIS enthuses: "Tony Flood has come up with virtually an A to Z of so many showbiz and sports stars from Peter Andre to David Walliams - and tells great stories about them! Fans young and old should love it."

Former world boxing champion FRANK BRUNO says: "Former journalist Tony Flood recalls some knockout anecdotes about his meetings with me and Muhammad Ali. He also has plenty of stories about George Best, Bobby Moore, Bobby Charlton, Harry Redknapp, Kenny Dalglish, Sir Alex Ferguson, Elvis Presley, Eric Morecambe, Joan Collins, Frank Sinatra, Kylie Minogue and many more!"

Comedian TIM VINE declares: "Tony Flood's book is full of funny and fascinating anecdotes from his many brushes with the rich and famous. Above all, what shines through is his love of the crazy world of entertainment and the extraordinary people in it."

Soccer legend MALCOLM MACDONALD, who disagrees with Alan Shearer in this new edition on who is the greatest Premiership team ever, says:

"Tony Flood, the former editor of Football Monthly and a Sky Television executive, has so many interesting and amusing tales to tell about big names from soccer, other sports and showbiz. He worked alongside one of the all time greats in Bobby Moore, and even got to play with Bobby, George Best and myself - which helped Tony to pick up the inside stories."

Actor BRIAN CAPRON, a Coronation Street legend, proclaims: "Journalist Tony Flood provides more startling secrets and hilarious anecdotes about showbiz and sports stars in the second edition of his celebrity book My Life With The Stars.

They include Eric Morecambe, Kylie Minogue, Brian Conley, The Spice Girls, more Elvis Presley revelations... plus some advice for Simon Cowell! One of many comedy gems explains why howls of laughter greeted my dramatic murder scene as serial killer Richard Hillman in Coronation Street. Tony's book, which also features George Best, Muhammad Ali and soccer's treble winners, is a great read which should not be missed!"

Actor DANIEL HILL, who starred as retirement home manager Harvey Bains in 'Waiting for God', says: "Tony Flood's excellent celebrity book My Life With The Stars has revelations leaping out of every page!

Tony was a top Fleet Street journo' who's met them all...and this terrific book shows it!"

Former Manchester United manager TOMMY DOCHERTY says: "Tony Flood reveals more fascinating secrets about top sports and showbiz stars in the new edition of his excellent, well written and comprehensively researched book. The great stories about former Liverpool, Manchester United and other managers, Bobby Moore, George Best and Muhammad Ali etc., make riveting and very amusing reading.

My Life With The Stars also gives a new insight into many of the scandals that have gone on in the world of sport, show business and newspapers.

And there are some rib-tickling quotes from Harry Redknapp and yours truly. This book should appeal to everyone, men and women, young and old. Once you start reading it you can't put it down."

MORE ENDORSEMENTS APPEAR AT THE END OF THE BOOK FROM WELL KNOWN PERSONALITIES.

CONTENTS

PREFACE

This new edition of My Life with the Stars adds revelations and updates about more showbiz and sports icons, including Eric Morecambe, David Walliams, Rowan Atkinson, Kylie Minogue, Peter Andre, Brian Conley, Des O'Connor, Bruce Forsyth and Harry Redknapp plus the contrasting views of Alan Shearer and Malcolm Macdonald on the Manchester City triple winners.

I've written about, interviewed or chatted to a galaxy of stars during my long career as a journalist, television executive, author and theatre critic.

So this book also features Elvis Presley, Frank Sinatra, Joan Collins, The Spice Girls and a host of other show business personalities. The most charismatic sporting characters I've met have been George Best and Muhammad Ali.

Meeting my two super heroes was a great privilege and also brought me into contact with two glamorous ladies who were offering to have sex with them! That is why the original edition of My Life with the Stars had the supplementary title 'Best, Ali and the panties'. There are now some startling panty revelations about Elvis to add to those concerning Best and Ali in this edition!

Other sports stars did not seem to have the same effect on the ladies, but I had some fascinating interviews with football greats Sir Bobby Charlton, Sir Stanley Matthews and Sir Tom Finney, boxers Frank Bruno, Henry Cooper and Nigel Benn, golfers Tony Jacklin and Sandy Lyle and tennis player Monica Seles. And there have been clashes with Kenny Dalglish and Alan Curbishley which I'll also tell you about later.

The kindest and most helpful actor I've met may surprise you because he played the much hated psycho Richard Hillman in Coronation Street. Yes, it's Brian Capron, who is a lovely guy.

The most delightful actresses have been June Whitfield, who sadly passed away at the age of 93, Shirley Anne Field, Susan Penhaligon, Linda Gray from 'Dallas', Patsy Kensit, Kate O'Mara and the lovely Joanne Heywood and Susie Amy.

June was a real sweetie, who rarely had a bad word to say about anyone, but she told me why her demanding television partner Terry Scott gave some actors a difficult time.

A sex symbol who did not send my pulse racing was Abi Titmuss (as bright as a button, pleasant and admittedly attractive, but not the glamour girl I had expected).

Singers oozing star quality when we chatted have been Dec Cluskey of the Bachelors, who, like Brian Capron, has been a great help to me, Petula Clark, Clare Sweeney, Cher, Mark Wynter (now an actor), Anita Harris and the late Max Bygraves...the list goes on!

A young Max Bygraves used to sing in the public house run by my grandparents in Woolwich, South East London, long before he was famous. I met him years later in Yarmouth and reminded him about it, but I omitted to tell him that, after hearing him perform in their pub, my grandparents didn't think he would ever become a star!

Tony gets a helping hand from Patsy Kensit

I have not met Sinatra, The Beatles, Joan Collins or Peter Sellers, but I have some great stories about them in this book thanks to my contacts in the world of show business. I will be revealing Sinatra's darker side; why Paul McCartney peed on his rival's shoes; how Joan Collins' words led to co-star Kate O'Mara being axed from 'Dynasty'; why Sellers made his wife Britt Ekland squirm with embarrassment; and how Elvis irritated Tom Jones.

During my time as Controller of Information at Sky Television, I had to sort out various problems, two of which concerned snooker star Jimmy White and football manager Ron Atkinson (more details later!).

Most days at Sky I was rubbing shoulders with the likes of Lennox Lewis, Ryder Cup golfer Brian Barnes, Roger Black, who won 4x400metre relay gold medals at both the World and European Championships, World snooker champion Dennis Taylor and Eurosport's head of programmes Adrian Metcalfe, a former Olympic Games athlete.

I also interviewed on camera Jimmy White, Stephen Hendry and Barry Hearn while helping to organise one of Sky and Eurosport's biggest sports events, the first World Snooker Masters.

I frequently mixed with Bobby Moore when I was his boss at the notorious down-market tabloid Sunday Sport, but a few of the celebrities I met might not even remember my name because I was not a famous columnist, although I wrote by-lined double-page spreads for the Daily Mirror, Sunday Mirror, The People and Daily Star as a freelance.

Several years of my career were spent in executive roles as Editor of Football Monthly magazine, Controller of Information at Sky Television, Sports Editor of the Lancashire Evening Telegraph Series and, of course, Head of Sport at Sunday Sport, and later the Fleet Street News Agency.

But at the news agency I was in effect a freelance writer who earned by-lines with various national, regional and weekly newspapers by interviewing many big name stars and snatching quotes from others, usually either before or after top sports events.

There are some great anecdotes to recall. I even got invited to put my hand on the bare thigh of 'Strictly Come Dancing's Miss Whiplash, Erin Boag!

In addition to working as a television public relations executive at Sky, my career as a journalist over more than 45 years included an enjoyable spell as editor of Football Monthly, Britain's oldest football magazine. I later worked on the staff of national Sunday tabloid paper The People part-time until September, 2010 when I finally retired.

There have also been appearances on radio and television, including featuring regularly on BBC News 24 as a sports pundit. If you missed me that was because they stuck me on at 6.30 in the morning!

I have been given some interesting missions as a writer, including acting as a stand-up comedian!

I was able to tell my audience that I was the first journalist in the family, in stark contrast to my great grandfather, who was a floor stainer - he didn't mean to be, but as he got older he couldn't help himself! Boom, boom!

Other journalistic tasks saw me take dancing lessons from the delightful Erin Boag, climb the Great Wall of China, organise and judge a beauty competition and play football with George Best and Bobby Moore.

Scoring a goal against a star-studded team which included Ossie Ardiles and Steve Coppell has got to be a highlight.

Since 'retiring' to Eastbourne I have got to know Brian Capron, Batchelors star Dec Cluskey and Shirley Anne Field.

Dec kindly introduced the film premiere of the comedy play I wrote called 'Hacking It' when it was shown at the Winter Garden Theatre, Eastbourne in 2012, and Shirley Anne sent a wonderful 'good luck' message to be read out to the audience. Brian Capron and best-selling author Tamara McKinley, who also writes under 'Ellie Dean', have kindly launched books for both myself and my wife Heather, author of the Mousey Mousey series and other children's books.

Let me start by telling you about the man, who for me, was the greatest footballer and playboy in the world!

CHAPTER ONE

George Best and the G-string

I met George Best a couple of times socially and on the second occasion I was asked by one of his sexy female admirers to hand him her G-string, wrapped around a key, so that she could try to lure him into her bedroom.

But my biggest memory of Best was playing with him in a benefit match for former Charlton Athletic goal-scoring hero Derek Hales. I will relate this amusing story first and come to the foxy lady a little later!

My appearance with the Irish genius was also memorable for another Charlton player, Steve Gritt, who later became the club's joint manager.

Gritt wrote in the club programme: "It was a massive coup to get George along. The one thing I remember about the game was that a reporter called Tony Flood came on at half-time and followed George around for 45 minutes. It was like he was shadow-marking him - but they were on the same team!"

That's how much in awe of Best I was at the time!

He had lost his acceleration, but I was able to see his magic footwork at close hand as he glided past opponents as if they weren't there. It was a master class in ball control and, needless to say, there were several goals created or scored that day by the former Manchester United legend, arguably the greatest player of his era.

George Best with team-mate Tony and Tony's son James

I don't think I contributed much, apart from one 'golden' moment. I actually played a return pass to Best to help set up one of the goals, which left me well chuffed! I was extremely grateful to the organiser Michael La Roche for inviting me to play in this star-studded match at Welling United's ground on May 5, 1985, simply on the basis that I was reasonably well known locally as a journalist who covered Charlton's matches.

My other team-mates and I saw Best naked in the showers afterwards - and he still looked in pretty good shape to us, even though he was well past his prime and loved drinking.

But my admiration for George was nothing compared to what the ladies felt for him. I was present on another occasion when a leggy lady went to great lengths to get him into her bed.

We were at a plush hotel where I chatted to George in a 'VIP area' which was out of bounds to this very attractive, elegantly dressed woman who called "Hello, George" in a deliciously soft voice. All she got from Bestie was a smile, but that did not deter her.

This gorgeous blonde, in her thirties, watched me go to the loo and presumably she quickly visited the 'ladies' at the same time. When I came out of the 'gents' she was waiting for me.

She pressed herself against me, pushed something into my hand and purred seductively with that wonderful voice: "Give this to George - tell him it's from the blonde he smiled at." When I looked I found she had given me her bright pink G-string, with the waistband tied around a room key.

Without a trace of embarrassment she smiled at me mischievously, and then added: "Tell him I've just taken it off."

George laughed about such incidents and revealed that so many women propositioned him he lost count. This illustrates just how much of a magnet Best was to the opposite sex - even when he was no longer playing. At least he then had no obligations to any club and was free to do what he liked. Unfortunately, his sex romps were probably even more frequent during the time he was supposed to be at peak fitness at Manchester United.

The worst example of his sexual exploits came when he was caught in the act by his then manager Wilf McGuinness at the team's hotel on the afternoon of Manchester United's FA Cup semi-final against Leeds in 1970.

An attractive woman had come into contact with Best on the hotel's stairs and he wasted no time in persuading her to go to his room.

McGuinness wanted to send him home, but Sir Matt Busy persuaded his young successor to let Best play - against Wilf's better judgement.

"George had an absolute nightmare of a game," McGuinness recalled. "We drew 0-0 and George missed the chance to win it for us by falling over the ball in front of goal." Two years earlier Best had been one of the heroes of United's European Cup final triumph.

I felt sorry for George because temptation was constantly put in front of him everywhere he went - something which his Manchester United team-mates Bobby Charlton, Denis Law and Co. were not exposed to in the same way.

Girls screamed whenever George made a personal appearance, and we had to stop them from molesting him at the testimonial football match!

Older women were also smitten by him. Actress Barbara Windsor, famous for her big boobs and saucy roles in the Carry On films, was one of them.

She explained how females of all ages were captivated by his amazing sex appeal, which was nothing short of animal magnetism.

Barbara, who freely admitted having 'a magic moment' with Best, asked challengingly when interviewed by Piers Morgan: "How many women would have said 'no' to him? He was so beautiful.

"I met him at the premiere of a 'Carry On' in Manchester. In the bar afterwards he came over to me and I told him: 'Don't waste your time with me, darling, when all those lovely ladies are after you'.

"He said: 'When do I ever get to talk to someone like you?' So that was it, a 'magic moment' again."

Barbara, who also had flings with Maurice Gibb from the Bee Gees, co-star Sid James and notorious gangsters Reggie and Charlie Kray, did not go into detail about her experience with Bestie. But she added: "He was fabulous!"

Best liked women of all shapes and sizes and Barbara was certainly all shapes and sizes! The actress was only 4ft 11in tall, but had a 36C bust, of which she said: "I wasn't always the confident, feisty blonde - two of my greatest assets were the bane of my life."

Tony with George Best

George, who started out as a tongue-tied shy lad from Belfast but rapidly grew in confidence, liked to share some great anecdotes. My favourite was when he was staying in a plush hotel and a bellboy delivered some champagne to his luxury room where George was entertaining a scantily-clad Miss World on a bed covered with his winnings from a casino.

The bellboy said. "May I ask you a question, Mr. Best? Where did it all go wrong?"

George had such an impish sense of humour. The Manchester United idol, who drove his managers mad with his disappearing acts, admitted: "I used to go missing a lot - Miss Canada, Miss United Kingdom, Miss World..."

There was usually a touch of truth about his jokes. This was certainly the case when he confessed: "I spent 90 per cent of my money on women and drink - the rest I wasted."

Alcohol was George's downfall and led to him spending eight weeks in prison for drink driving and an assault on a policeman from December 1984. He recalled how while he was in prison he and his then girlfriend Angie Lynn used to indulge in postal sex by writing 'obscene' letters to each other "detailing what we planned to do to one another in bed when I got out." He tells the full story in 'George Best Blessed – The Autobiography'

There are also many more stories about Bestie in 'George Best: A Memoir', 'Immortal' and 'George and Me: My Autobiography' by Angie Best and Nicola Pittam.

George and his loyal, kind-hearted first wife Angie were the Victoria and David Beckham of their time after marrying in Las Vegas on January 24th, 1978, but they divorced in 1986 following George's problems with alcohol abuse and womanising.

The delightful Angie has been most helpful to me.

George married the equally devoted Alex Pursey in 1995, but more heavy drinking - and domestic violence - led to them divorcing in 2004, a year before George died, aged only 59.

CHAPTER TWO

Showbiz pals were targets for Eric Morecambe's impish fun

Eric Morecambe had a wicked sense of humour, both on and off stage. And some of his showbiz friends were on the receiving end, particularly Des O'Connor.

Des O'Connor giving me some good advice

When I met Des and watched him perform in Eastbourne he revealed Eric's biggest 'put down'. He recalled: "I once told Eric I had done a one-man show and he replied 'Let's hope two turn up next time'."

Fiona Castle, widow of popular entertainer Roy Castle, also tells how some of Eric's impish fun was at her expense after appearing with Morecambe and Wise at the Coventry Hippodrome where she was a dancer in the chorus.

Fiona, who was giving one of her talks when I met her at the Langham Hotel, Eastbourne, let slip to Eric that she was a big fan of the multi-talented Roy and would love to meet him. So some time later Eric invited her to a TV show to introduce her to Roy.

But he embarrassed her by saying: "Roy, this is Fiona, and she's in love with you."

She then learned that Eric had been even more outrageous when he had set up the meeting. He had told Roy: "I've got this sad little case coming to see you. She has braces and a pigtail - try to be nice to her."

Despite this awkward meeting between two shy people, Roy and Fiona hit it off so well they married a year later!

The charming Fiona, who has done a lot of excellent work for the Roy Castle Lung Cancer Foundation, is a talented author[*].

Behind every successful man is a great woman, as the saying goes - and in Eric Morecambe's case it was TWO great women.

His mother Sadie and his wife Joan both played major parts in his career. Sadie suggested that he team-up with Ernie Wise to form one of the greatest ever comedy double acts, and Joan gave up her own showbiz career to enhance his.

Eric's daughter Gail, who I had the pleasure of meeting when she gave a talk at Warner's Holiday Centre at Sinah Warren in Hayling Island, and his son Gary* have both played glowing tributes to Sadie and Joan.

Gail said: "Sadie was an extraordinary woman. She took Dad to auditions and encouraged him to form the partnership with Ernie that saw their careers take off."

Another big influence was Joan Bartlett. She took over from a dancer who became ill at the Empire Theatre, Edinburgh - and found herself working with Eric and Ernie. A year later, in December 1952, she and Eric got married.

Gail recalled: "Mum's career stopped and she became Dad's support system. Dad was fully aware he could not have achieved half of what he did without her."

* *Fiona Castle is author of GIVE US THIS DAY, NO FLOWERS...JUST LOTS OF JOY and compiler of several anthologies including RAINBOWS THROUGH THE RAIN, WHAT A WONDERFUL WORLD and LET ME COUNT THE WAYS. She also wrote Topic of Cancer with Jan Greenough.*

* *Several books have been written about Morecambe and Wise, including 'Morecambe & Wise: 50 Years of Sunshine' by Gary Morecambe*

CHAPTER THREE

Ali and the nude photo

Meeting Frank Bruno and Muhammad Ali were marvellous experiences and lots of fun!

I got to know Bruno, the much-loved former British and WBC heavyweight champion, pretty well when I was Head of Sport at Sunday Sport in the late 1980s.

We were both going to the Sports Personality of the Year dinner where I was helping to entertain sports stars such as Nick Faldo and Frank himself because I was a member of the committee of the Sports Writers Association who were making the awards.

The amiable Bruno and I bumped into each other as we approached the Wembley venue.

Frank said to me: "Hello, Mr. Sunday Sport." Then he told me: "I'm worried because I've forgotten to bring my ticket. There might be a problem, know what I mean?"

I assured Frank that the officials would let him in, especially as everyone would recognise him. I was right on the first count but wrong on the second.

When we got to the reception area there was my date, a charming but perhaps on occasions a slightly 'dizzy' lady called Linda. I said to her: "Hi Linda. Let me introduce you to Frank."

She looked at him without a flicker of recognition and replied: "Hello Frank. Do you work with Tony, then?

Linda must have been the only person in the building, probably the whole country, who didn't seem to know who the giant, affable man in front of her really was.

Frank showed tremendous bravery in the ring, especially when he lost to Mike Tyson in five punishing rounds in their first world title clash in February 1989. But his biggest fight was to overcome the bipolar disorder which led to him being sectioned. When he recovered, he decided to set up The Frank Bruno Foundation, a charity running boxing and well-being programmes to help children, young people and adults cope with mental health issues.

Bruno speaks out to show there is no shame in asking for help with mental health problems in his book 'Let Me Be Frank', published in May, 2018.

I loved my chats with the larger than life Bruno, who does not come far behind Muhammad Ali as the most charismatic boxer I ever interviewed.

That happened in August, 1966 after Ali had come to England to defend his World Heavyweight Championship against Brian London, who he knocked out in the third round at Earl's Court Exhibition Hall.

London liked to 'boss' his opponents, but he seemed apprehensive against Ali, whose speed of punching was truly amazing.

As you may recall, Ali would dance away from his opponents and catch them with his lightning fast long left hand. So London was forced to go reluctantly forward, but with the air of a cautious man who maybe felt it would be better to back away. Not surprisingly, Ali soon put him out of his misery.

Ali 'entertained' the Press afterwards and I was among those who got to meet the great man - a privilege denied to hundreds of fans milling around the hall.

One of them was an attractive brunette in the shortest of mini shirts which showed off her amazingly long and shapely legs.

A security man saw me looking at her and said to me: "She's really something, isn't she? She has just given me this envelope to pass on to Ali."

He had already checked its contents, apparently. Now, he opened it completely and there inside was a nude photo of the brunette, dangling her panties tantalisingly between forefinger and thumb, with her phone number scrawled on the back!

We looked across at her and at least she had the decency to blush!

The security man added: "She's wasting her time. Even if I had the nerve to give the photo to Ali, there's no way I'd be stupid enough to do so with all you Press guys around and the TV cameras recording everything!"

The cameras had certainly picked up London's discomfort as he was out-classed and out-fought. He was later to admit that he decided to quit in the third round because he didn't want to risk ending up punch-drunk. London said: "I got paid the same for three rounds as I would have for 15."

I asked Ali why he was so boastful - was it merely to hype up fights against lesser lights like London or was it to unnerve his opponents? He replied, with a grin: "It's hard to be humble when you're as great as I am."

Despite his total arrogance and brashness, Ali had me and most of the other normally cynical journalists eating out of his hand with his wit, charm, charisma and sheer magnetism.

Ali, previously known as Cassius Clay, had changed his name in 1964 immediately after taking the title, against all the odds, from the ferocious Sonny Liston.

His title shot had almost been ruined when he fought Britain's Henry Cooper at Wembley in 1963. An over-confident Clay was caught by Henry's hammer in a sensational fourth round and seemed to be heading for defeat, but his corner man Angelo Dundee bought him more time to recover between rounds by deliberately enlarging a split in his glove.

Contrary to popular belief, Dundee did not split the glove with a razor. A small tear in the glove had occurred earlier so what the quick-thinking Dundee did was to put his finger into it and make it far worse.

By the time Dundee's demands for a new glove had been sorted out, Clay had recovered and avoided the defeat which might have wrecked all his big money world title plans.

Dundee had already violated the British boxing rules by appearing to use smelling salts to revive Clay in his corner.

The fifth round saw Cassius take full advantage of his let off. He unleashed a lightning fast right hand punch which opened a severe cut under Cooper's eye, causing referee Tommy Little to stop the fight.

Clay confided afterwards: "Cooper's left hand so nearly knocked me out. He hit me so hard that my ancestors in Africa felt it. If the bell hadn't sounded for the end of the round immediately after I got up, then he could have finished the job."

But Cooper felt he would have nailed his man with that one punch if the ropes had not intervened. He revealed: "Unfortunately, the ropes cushioned his fall. If I had hit him away from the ropes perhaps he would have been counted out."

In 1966 Cooper had a re-match at Highbury with the renamed Ali, by then world heavyweight champion. Accumulated scar tissue around Cooper's eyes made him even more vulnerable than in the previous contest and a serious cut was opened up by Ali's constant jabs, which led to the fight being stopped.

Fans were divided about Ali's pre-fight boasts of what he would do to opponents and which round he would beat them in.

But it was all hype. As Ali revealed: "The more I boasted, the more the fans got stirred up and the more tickets they bought to see me."

My Press colleagues and I picked up some great quotes from Ali. He proclaimed: "A man who views the world the same at 50 as he did at 20 wasted 30 years of his life."

Muhammad had me in stitches with his boasts. He claimed: "I'm so fast that last night I turned off the light switch and was in bed before the room was dark."

And he insisted: "My toughest fight was with my first wife."

My friend Harry Higgins can echo that. When Harry divorced his wife the judge told him "I've heard all the evidence, Mr. Higgins, and I'm going to give Mrs. Higgins £1,000 a month." Harry replied: "That's very nice of you, Your Honour, I'll try to chip in a few bob myself."

CHAPTER FOUR

What Sinatra expected from Shirley Anne

I got on friendly terms with Shirley Anne Field, one of the most glamorous British starlets ever to graduate to full blown super stardom on the big screen.

My wife Heather and I met her briefly after she gave a fascinating talk, accompanied by film clips of her starring movie roles, to an appreciative audience of Friends of the Devonshire Park Theatre members in Eastbourne in December, 2011.

We later took her to afternoon tea and exchanged emails as well as having a couple of chats on the phone - and I have found her to be a lovely, kind lady.

Shirley Anne spoke frankly with warmth, grace and humour about her private and professional life during her talk in the Congress Suite, Eastbourne and also told a fantastic story about her date with Frank Sinatra.

Ol' Blue Eyes, at the time the biggest star in the world, was apparently expecting more from her than she was prepared to give after he phoned the then19-year-old starlet and asked her to be his date when he came to London. He inquired if she 'liked to party' and she said she did, not realising what Sinatra meant by that.

The singer sent Shirley Anne a dress and jewellery to wear.

He introduced her to a host of celebrities, including Mrs Peter Lawford, sister of John F. Kennedy, and Shirley Anne nervously dropped champagne over her twice!

Shirley Anne Field poses with Tony and his wife Heather (right)

Frank's charm was replaced by anger when photographers burst into a nightclub to picture them because he incorrectly thought the young actress had tipped off the Press.

Shirley Anne wanted to go home but was told by Sinatra's minders that she could not leave until he did.

At the end of her nightmare date with the demanding and controlling show business legend, the minders asked her to give back the dress and jewellery. She threw the jewellery at them but said she was not taking off the dress.

Later she realised she should have given them the dress but kept the jewellery! At least she left with her honour intact!

Shirley Anne also described in her book 'A Time For Love' her tough upbringing in a children's home in Lancashire where they cut off her lovely long hair, with the aid of a pudding basin.

But she survived with a combination of courage, determination and charm - three of the qualities that were to make her a top film star.

Shirley Anne, who had to wake up at 4am each day to be at the studios, landed the part of a beauty queen to play opposite Sir Laurence Olivier in 'The Entertainer'.

She then starred in 'Saturday Night and Sunday Morning' with Albert Finney and 'Alfie' with Michael Caine. It changed her life, and the girl from Bolton was wined and dined by the likes of Richard Burton, David Niven and Warren Beatty as she made the transition from starlet to respected actress.

In recent years she has appeared in stage plays and given talks about her fascinating life. But she still found time to encourage me with my writing of children's novels, this book and a comedy script.

The thoughtful Shirley Anne sent me a lovely good luck message to be read out at the film premiere of my comedy 'Hacking It', which has nothing to do with the telephone hacking that brought down The News Of The World. In fact, the oddball characters in the zany local newspaper office I created in my play are so inept that they would think it an achievement to dial a telephone number correctly!

Shirley Anne wrote: "To my new friend Tony Flood, wishing you the best of luck with the film premiere of 'Hacking It'. It is a rather appropriate title in view of the fact that you have recently had your computer hacked into. Hope you and your executive director Alan Baker have every success by turning 'Hacking It' into a TV sitcom (with parts for all of us!).

"Thank you for your books - I am reading 'The Secret Potion' and enjoying it."

CHAPTER FIVE

Top funny men take comedy seriously

Funny men Norman Wisdom, David Jason, Rowan Atkinson, Stephen Fry and Benny Hill have taken comedy very seriously.

This was revealed to me by Brian Conley and actor Denis Lill, who appeared in two episodes of Blackadder. It was backed up by Bruce Forsyth, Nicholas Parsons and Tony Robinson (the loveable Baldrick in Blackadder).

Brian Conley told me: "Comedy legends who wrote and performed sketches like Benny Hill, Norman Wisdom and Charlie Chaplin were dedicated to their craft and felt that the harder you rehearsed the better you made the end product. Getting the delivery and timing just right is vital."

Bruce Forsyth said Norman Wisdom was meticulous about scripts and insisted they stick to the script when performing their famous wallpapering sketch at the London Palladium in December, 1961.

In 'Bruce The Autobiography', Forsyth revealed: "He insisted on every line being delivered exactly as it was written, with no deviation whatsoever."

So Bruce, who worked as hard as anyone in rehearsals but liked to ad-lib, found in his sketch with Wisdom that the written line couldn't be changed in any way.

Morecambe and Wise were more flexible, though just as serious about rehearsals. Ernie said that very little of their routine contained ad libs, but he explained: "We would have done about three or four versions in rehearsals and the 'ad libs' came from those versions."

TV viewers remember Benny Hill as a saucy, fun-loving rascal chasing after scantily-clad attractive girls on set, but he was a perfectionist.

Nicholas Parsons, who worked on The Benny Hill Show in the late 1960s, said in 'Nicholas Parsons - With Just a Touch of Hesitation, Repetition and Deviation: My Life in Comedy' how the comedian had definite ideas on the role of his straight man.

Parsons recalled that Benny never liked him playing for laughs in character. "He had a charming way of letting me know. 'Oh, Nicky, Nicky, don't go for the laugh there, darling boy. Just play it straight'."

Denis Lill, who was Rodney Trotter's Father-in-law in Only Fools and Horses, told me: "Comedy stars can become obsessed with getting things just right. When we were filming Only Fools and Horses, David Jason wanted to do as many 'takes' as necessary to get a scene as good as we possibly could.

"David had worked with a real master in Ronnie Baker, who had given him a very good education.

"It was the same with Rowan Atkinson and Co. on Blackadder. Rowan and David are cast in the same mould and believe that comedy is a serious business. When you're filming there's no time to lark around."

Tony Robinson revealed: "Every line in the rehearsal script was challenged by the Blackadder cast. Tim McInnerny or Stephen Fry or Hugh Laurie or Rowan would be asking 'how can we make this better?'"

Richard Curtis, who wrote the scripts, first with Atkinson and later with Ben Elton, added that this was difficult and testing but effective.

One of the most dedicated - and helpful - comedians was Ken Dodd, as squeaky-voiced Joe Pasquale confirmed to me.

At the start of Joe's TV career, he appeared on talent show New Faces back in 1987 and on the panel of judges was Doddy, already a national comedy treasure.

Joe had to audition off camera in the afternoon to see if he was going on the show itself, and Ken's support helped put him through. A grateful Joe recalled: "Ken saw me backstage and gave me advice on how to improve my act and get more laughs. I did what he said and it put me on the way to the final where I came second."

Sir Ken, master of tickling sticks, Diddy Men and tattifilarious comedy, was a sad loss when he died, aged 90.

Nicholas Parsons told me he believed that, at 94, he was the oldest person working regularly in show business, and had no intention of retiring.

He said: "I love my profession and have never considered retiring. My legs are weaker and I need a stick, but I'll keep going as long as I've got the mental stamina and the ability to perform. If you use your grey matter it keeps you young."

Most comedians tour extensively but dread playing in front of demanding Glaswegian audiences. Des O'Connor recalled: "I fainted with fear at the Glasgow Empire. I just went down in a heap after going on stage. Eric Morecambe said to me 'You're the only comic who's sold advertising space on the soles of your shoes'."

My favourite joke was told by Bob Monkhouse, who quipped: "They laughed when I said I was going to be a comedian...they're not laughing now."

Ken Dodd almost topped that with his jibes at the tax man after walking free from Liverpool Crown Court in 1989, having been acquitted on all eight charges in his tax fraud trial.

He jested: "In the 1800s, an MP decided to introduce tax. In those days it was 2p in the pound - I thought it still was."

Doddy came up with another gem about life in the Garden of Eden. Eve asked Adam if he loved her and he replied "You're the only one for me."

But some of the best comic moments are unintended.

Brian Capron could not understand why the cast and crew of Coronation Street burst out laughing after he had played one of his most dramatic scenes as serial killer Richard Hillman.

He told me: "It was the murder of Maxine where I delivered the famous line 'You should have stayed at the party Maxine!'

"After the horrific murder I came off set to howls of laughter, because, when clearing the top of a cabinet to make it look like a robbery, I had inadvertently knocked a cordless telephone up into the air and it had landed plum in between the 'dead' Tracy Shaw's bum cheeks !"

Unfortunately, Corrie viewers never saw this comedy gem. Brian explained: "Maxine's body wasn't shown until her husband found her in the next episode and the phone had been removed."

When it comes to visual slapstick humour, I think Laurel and Hardy were the greatest.

It was a tragedy that in their later years they found themselves often playing to half-empty theatres on their farewell eight-month British tour spanning parts of 1953 and 1954.

This was highlighted in the excellent film Stan & Ollie in which John C Reilly and Steve Coogan give brilliant performances while playing a wonderful, touching tribute to the legendary duo.

CHAPTER SIX

Kylie and Peter Andre talk about their breakdowns

The best advice I've ever been given by a big name star was from Des O'Connor. And I also try to take heed of some shrewd remarks by Peter Andre and Kylie Minogue.

When I met Des after he had performed in his one-man show at the Congress Theatre in Eastbourne in 2014 he gave me a wonderful tip. He said: "People worry too much about too many things. We should learn to only fret when something happens, rather than if something might happen, because half the things that you worry about in your life are never going to happen anyway."

Des, a mere 82 at the time, won us over with his self-deprecating humour. He recounted putting up with Eric Morecambe's jokes about him for 14 years; how he dated Shirley Bassey; played squash with Tom Jones and toured with Buddy Holly.

Kylie's advice fitted in very well with that of Mr O'Connor - getting stressed doesn't help!

She said: "I wish I hadn't stressed as much or had such insecurity at times." After her split from former fiancé Joshua Sasse, she told the Sydney Morning Herald: "I wish

I had trusted my instincts on some occasions when I didn't and I'd listened to better advice."

The glamorous Aussie, still regarded as a pop princess despite becoming 50 on May 28, 2018 and finding happiness with British GQ magazine boss Paul Solomons, revealed she had suffered a form of nervous breakdown after her split from Sasse.

Kylie, who also had relationships with actor Olivier Martinez, tragic INXS frontman Michael Hutchence and Neighbours co-star Jason Donovan, was devastated at discovering that Sasse was having an affair with a co-star at the end of 2016.

She told Stellar magazine: "It actually was nervous breakdown time. It ended up being not so much about heartbreak and more about stress."

Kylie was diagnosed with breast cancer at the age of 36 during her relationship with Martinez. She reflected that it's years until you really get the all-clear and "when my hair started growing back it was like a miracle."

Does Kylie sympathise with those women who try to beat the aging process? She told Elle magazine: "I've tried Botox. I'm definitely not one of those people who says, 'You shouldn't do this'."

Peter Andre revealed how he bounced back from a mental breakdown that nearly sunk his career.

The 46-year-old singer, who had previously enjoyed fame, acclaim and sex romps, said: "I suffered anxiety and depression, but I learned to face my fears and overcome them. Other sufferers can recover, too."

He had previously disclosed to the Mirror how the world tours, the success in Europe and the unbelievable amount of sex was replaced by hate. In Australia, people - guys particularly - absolutely hated him. There were even death threats.

"I tried to bury my fears and run away from it all but eventually it just all caught up with me and I broke down."

Peter, born in England of loving Greek parents who were devout Jehovah's Witnesses, had been raised in Australia and suffered bullying.

So his life has been full of ups and downs, both as a child and an adult. It has been well documented how Peter survived a difficult break up with his ex-wife Katie Price after four years of marriage which ended in 2009, but he has been happily married to Emily MacDonagh since 2015.

One of the most enjoyable interviews I've conducted in recent years was with Brian Conley.

The 57-year-old multi-talented star told him how he loves show-business and has been able to resist - or overcome - its temptations.

A drinking habit took its toll following the death of his much loved father Colin at the age of 59 from bowel cancer in 1998. Brian revealed: "Some nights I'd drink a bottle of wine and three Jim Beams. I was on stage one evening in 2003, after a bender the night before, and found myself stammering. I felt woolly. Although I was never an alcoholic, I had to give up drinking and haven't had an alcoholic drink in 15 years."

Brian Conley (centre) with Heather and me back stage

Brian's words of wisdom, which should be heeded by all addicts, are: "Resisting the desire to have a single drink is so important. It was the hardest thing I've ever done, but the most rewarding."

Another cause for alarm came when Brian had to quit 'I'm A Celebrity...Get Me Out of Here' through illness in November 2012. He recalled: "I went nine days in the jungle without proper food and had stopped taking anti-depressants which I'd been on for some years. Helen Flanagan kept failing her tasks to win food - if brains were taxed she'd be due a rebate."

So did he prefer Strictly Come Dancing on which he appeared in 2017? "Yes," he told me. "They fed us and it was such a popular show."

Brian, who to me is Britain's greatest living entertainer, started in showbiz at the age of 12. After lying about his age to get a job as a Pontins blue coat five years later, he broke into television as a warm-up man for Kenny Everett, Terry Wogan, Noel Edmonds and Russ Abbott.

The Paddington-born lad, the son of a cab driver and dinner lady, has given outstanding performances in eight musicals, including 'Me and My Girl', 'The Music Man' and 'Jolson'.

Brian has been very happily married to wife Anne-Marie since 1996. He wore a suit of armour to propose to her, and after the ceremony the couple left in a Chitty Chitty Bang Bang car.

He still worships Anne-Marie and was never tempted to succumb to the Strictly curse. "My wife's very special. We fit like a hand in a glove. You'd never want to give that up for a one-night stand."

Many in showbiz do have affairs, of course, particularly some of those in Strictly, and Bruce Forsyth admitted that he was unfaithful to his then wife Penny.

CHAPTER SEVEN

Fan told Grobbelaar: 'They're killing us'

The most emotional story I ever wrote was when I obtained an exclusive interview with Liverpool goalkeeper Bruce Grobbelaar the day after the Hillsborough disaster which was the deadliest stadium-related tragedy in British history.

It resulted in the deaths of 96 people on April 15th, 1989 at the FA Cup semi-final between Liverpool and Nottingham Forest which was abandoned after six minutes.

Grobbelaar was choking back the tears as he told me how he was trying to take a goal kick when a fan yelled at him: "Bruce, help us. They're killing us."

The goalkeeper asked who was killing them and the man replied: "Our own fans - they're crushing us against the fences." Grobbelaar told me: "A surge from the back was shoving fans forward and they were yelling to be let out. I asked the police to allow supporters to climb over the fences on to the areas surrounding the pitch while the game was still going on."

It was the most dramatic incident ever to happen during a major match.

The crush resulted from late-arriving Liverpool fans being allowed into the back of an already full stand at the Leppings Lane end of the ground.

Although the game was abandoned after six minutes, it was too late to save those who had been so severely crushed.

My exclusive interview with Grobbelaar made a double page spread in the Sunday Mirror.

Thousands more stories followed. Liverpool fans were blamed at first, but Lord Justice Taylor's initial inquiry found the primary cause of the fatalities was a failure of police control. Allegations that there had been a police 'cover up' emerged as bereaved families campaigned, and the aftermath of the tragedy has continued for 30 years, with charges brought against officials.

Journalists need to be persistent without being too intrusive. An example of this was when I agreed to do an interview with Sir Bobby Charlton for the Daily Express on the 40th anniversary of the Munich Air Disaster.

Charlton was one of the survivors of the air crash which killed 23 people when the Manchester United team was travelling back from a European Cup match in Belgrade, Yugoslavia against Red Star on February 6th, 1958.

Bobby had given me his telephone number but when I phoned him he said: "I'm sorry, Tony, but every year I get asked by journalists about this, and I'd rather not do an interview this time."

I was in a fix because the Daily Express was expecting 500 words from me. So I asked my wife Heather, who had no journalistic experience, to ring Bobby Charlton an hour later, saying she wanted to ask him some questions for a tribute article in memory of Jimmy Murphy, who had temporarily taken over the Manchester United team while manager Matt Busby was in hospital recovering from the plane crash.

I had written down six questions for Heather to put to him in the hope he would answer one or two of them. To my surprise Bobby gave full answers to all the questions, so I was able to write the article as a tribute to Murphy, which also, of course, reflected on the air crash.

Tony stands between sporting icons, Seb Coe and Sir Bobby Charlton

My only mistake was not giving Heather enough questions to ask Bobby! He was warming to his theme when she had to cut the conversation short because she'd run out of things to say!

Charlton recalled: "Jimmy Murphy kept the club afloat by cobbling together a team made up of reserves and loan players to help us complete our fixtures. Against all odds, he got us to the FA Cup final.

"Jimmy was a big influence on me. He told me that if there was space ahead of me to run with the ball, and that helped me to score some of my most memorable goals."

This is typical of Bobby - always quick to thank those who had played a part in his huge success story!

CHAPTER EIGHT

Joan Collins' words spelt the end for Kate

Joan Collins is a national institution, but the formidable British actress is not everyone's favourite person and I got the clear impression that was the case with the late Kate O'Mara, who starred with her in 'Dynasty', one of TV's biggest ever soap operas.

Kate O'Mara with Tony

It is hardly surprising because Kate revealed to me that Joan's remarks had led to her being axed from the show.

Joan had landed the starring role of the ruthless Alexis Colby in 1981, but the success enjoyed later in the series by fellow brunette Kate, who played Alexis's scheming sister Caress Morrell, may not have gone down well with her.

Kate recalled: "A Dynasty producer told me that Joan had said she didn't think it was a good idea to have two brunettes as the main characters in the show. It had apparently taken her two years to reach that conclusion.

"The upshot was that my character was swiftly shipped off to Australia and I was no longer in the show. They simply chose not to take up their option to extend my contract beyond two years.

"I don't know whether Joan might have felt threatened by me, but it was ironic that some of the best scenes in 'Dynasty' were those between us.

"If my success in 'Dynasty' did make Joan feel insecure, I suppose in some way it was a backhanded compliment to me."

Kate felt that the decision to axe her in 1988 rebounded on Joan. She explained: "Stephanie Beacham came into 'Dynasty' when I departed and she fires from both hips so I think Joan would have been better off continuing to work with me."

Joan, now 85, has aged remarkably well and benefited from not having any facial surgery or Botox.

Kate, who I found to be extremely friendly and helpful, did not undergo surgery, either, but admitted to having used Botox, which, in my view, rarely does users any favours.

Miss O'Mara said in a previous interview on Metro: "I've tried Botox, but I don't like it because it stops you being able to use your facial muscles, which, as an actress, are essential. But I do have collagen injections.

"I am fortunate in having this bone structure because I've got a tremendously prominent temple. I like to think that it's because I'm so intelligent.

"My teeth are my worst feature. I've hardly got any of my own left. I've got implants in my upper jaw and hardly any in my lower jaw and that is the problem.

"At one point I thought: 'I'm going to have to do a Marlon Brando and stuff some cotton wool in my mouth'."

Yet Ms O'Mara was in her element as a delightfully-snobbish elderly aunt at Devonshire Park Theatre, Eastbourne, in March, 2012 in Christie play 'Murder on the Nile', showing perfect timing while delivering some extremely funny put-downs.

Her equally charismatic co-stars, Susie Amy, from TV's 'Footballers Wives', and Denis Lill (Rodney's father-in-law in 'Only Fools and Horses'), were both generous in their praise of her.

Susie said: "Kate is absolutely terrific," while Denis added: "She's a delight to work with - she's reliable, remembers her lines and has bags of energy."

Joan Collins has a softer, loving side and is lavish in her praise of her fifth husband Percy Gibson, who is 31 years younger than her at 54.

It's great to have Susie Amy looking up to you

Mark Wynter, Tony, Susie and Denis Lill

Joan has always been outspoken and condemned the Hollywood casting couch following the Harvey Weinstein sexual harassment allegations.

She claimed to have been passed over for the role of Cleopatra because she wouldn't sleep with the studio head. Joan twice tested for the part, but it went to Elizabeth Taylor.

CHAPTER NINE

How I handled Bobby Moore

Bobby Moore is a soccer legend who proved himself to be a master at reading the game and making snap decisions when captaining England to their only World Cup triumph in 1966.

But when I worked with him I found that he sometimes wasn't the best at making decisions in everyday life!

I had been appointed head of sport at controversial tabloid Sunday Sport, with Bobby being given the title of Sports Editor, though the running of the operation was left to me. His duties included covering matches and writing a weekly column, but when asked to express his opinion on an issue Bobby often sat on the fence.

Sunday Sport's abrasive style was to come down heavily on one side of any argument, but Mr. Nice Guy Bobby would at times frustrate us, even when he seemed to offer a firm opinion, by then saying "But on the other hand...and giving the opposite view.

So I would patiently go through every aspect with him and count up how many 'pros' and 'cons' he came up with. Whatever was the highest would be printed in the paper as his rock solid opinion, with the other side of the coin ignored - and he accepted that.

Bobby was a very brave man, however, and he had secretly battled testicular cancer two years before he led England to World Cup triumph.

He remained a sporting icon and was still highly respected throughout the world. One day we received a letter in the office from Brazil, asking Bobby to play in a friendly involving veteran former soccer stars.

He told me he was not available, but asked if I would tell the Brazilians that two other members of England's World Cup winning side, his old West Ham team-mates Geoff Hurst and Martin Peters, probably would be.

I informed the Brazilian FA about this, but the message came back that they only wanted Bobby Moore. Even Hurst, our hat-trick hero against the Germans in that glorious World Cup final, was not considered to be in the same class as Moore!

Of course, the Brazilians still remembered how well Moore had performed against them in the 1970 World Cup, in which their star player Pele showed his respect for our captain by swapping shirts with him after helping Brazil to beat the holders 1-0.

Pele declared: "Of the hundreds of defenders who played against me during my career I pick Bobby Moore as the greatest of them all. He was also the fairest defender I ever played against."

Bobby returned the compliment. He told me: "Pele was the most complete player I've ever played against or ever seen. He was a great goal scorer and had amazing all-round skill plus a superb footballing brain."

So when they faced each other on the field a fantastic battle of wits resulted because Moore was the master defender, clinical in the tackle and strong in the air. He lacked pace, but read the game so well this was seldom a noticeable weakness.

Despite his great successes, Bobby's family experienced more bad fortune than good.

His first marriage to Tina ended in divorce, and she and his second wife Stephanie suffered an even more shattering blow with Bobby's death from cancer, aged 51, in 1993.

Tragedy struck again when Tina and Bobby's son Dean, who worked with Bobby and I at Sunday Sport as a youngster, died in July 2011, at the age of 43.

A popular and friendly member of staff while at the paper, he was a diabetic. He died after collapsing from a life-threatening complication of the disease, an inquest heard.

Dean, who also had a history of alcohol dependency, depression, gout and asthma, was found lying on the living room floor of his Notting Hill support centre by a care worker after his worried mother Tina had been unable to contact him.

His death meant the Moore family had lost a father, son, brother and uncle.

Bobby himself had his share of ill luck. It was in the build up to the 1970 World Cup that the England skipper was involved in one of the game's most controversial incidents.

Moore was accused of stealing a bracelet from a hotel shop in Bogota, Colombia.

A young assistant claimed that he had taken the bracelet without paying for it while accompanying Bobby Charlton in looking for a gift for Charlton's wife, Norma.

This sensational story continued to hog all the headlines as Moore was arrested and then released, but, after helping England win 2-0 against Ecuador in Qutom, he was placed under house arrest on returning to Colombia.

Diplomatic pressure, plus the fact there was no evidence against Moore, eventually saw the case dropped in time for him to play in the World Cup in Mexico.

No doubt 1970 was Bobby's worst ever year because on August 10 he received an anonymous threat to kidnap his wife Tina and hold her to a £10,000 ransom. This caused him to pull out of two pre-season friendlies

The West Ham legend liked a drink and this got him into trouble the following year. On January 7, 1971, he and three of his Hammers team-mates, Jimmy Greaves, Clyde Best and Brian Dear, were all fined by West Ham manager Ron Greenwood after going out drinking in a nightclub until the early hours of the morning prior to an FA Cup third round tie against bottom-of-the-table Blackpool, which they lost 4-0.

Moore had been voted the Player of Players when leading England to triumph in the 1966 World Cup, yet he almost missed out on what was to be his greatest triumph. Earlier that year he had seemed set to leave West Ham and let his contract expire.

It was pointed out that Moore would be ineligible to play in the World Cup because he was technically without a club. So England boss Sir Alf Ramsey called upon Greenwood to come to England's training camp at Hendon Hall and give Moore a one-month temporary contract with West Ham to cover the tournament. This allowed Bobby to lead England to glory.

But it appeared that Ramsey seriously considered leaving Moore out of the final.

The England manager had been overheard talking to his coaching staff about the possibility of dropping his skipper and using the more physical and mobile Norman Hunter in preference against the speedy German forwards. Fortunately, he stuck with his captain.

Appropriately, it was Moore's 40-yard perfect pass that set Hurst up for his hat-trick and England's fourth goal.

Moore opened doors for us at Sunday Sport, as was demonstrated when I put together an All Star team to play in charity matches. The fact he was captaining our Sunday Sport side meant I could persuade the likes of Emlyn Hughes, Malcolm Macdonald, George Graham and John Greig to play.

Tony gets the girl as the stars look on. Can you spot George Graham, Bobby Moore, Frank McLintock, Terry Naylor and the others?

Amazingly, the FA and most club bosses had shunned Bobby when he gave up playing which, as Tina revealed, caused him to slump into depression[*].

[*] *Tina tells all in her autobiography 'Bobby Moore: By the Person who Knew him Best' and there are other great stories about Bobby in 'Bobby Moore: The Man in Full' by Matt Dickinson and 'Bobby Moore: the Definitive Biography' and 'Bobby Moore Authorised Biography', both by Jeff Powell.*

CHAPTER TEN

Star-struck Elvis was an embarrassment

One of my contacts in show business told me that Elvis Presley was so much in awe of Tom Jones that he was like a star-struck fan.

Elvis also became an embarrassment to friends years later during the last 18 months of his life, when he was bloated, confused and liable to mood swings due to his dependency on prescription drugs.

It is claimed that the King of Rock 'n' Roll went from being the iconic figure everybody wanted to be with to a person some friends would cross the street to avoid. He then became reclusive and chose to be on his own.

I was first given an insight into the sad situation during one of my trips to Las Vegas. I was told that there had been signs in Presley's concert performances of his decline. He mumbled introductions, sang the wrong lyrics and looked uncoordinated in his movements on stage.

My contact, who has big show business connections but preferred to be unnamed, told me how embarrassing this was for Presley's friends.

He claimed: "Some stayed loyal and some did not, while Elvis pushed other friends away. He was sad that Tom Jones was no longer in the States. Presley had seemed to idolise Jones - just like a star-struck fan, to the point it became excessive."

Welsh heart-throb Tom said: "I didn't realise how ill he was. The first thing that hit me after he died was that I should have gone to see him."

The two singers had first met at the Paramount film set in 1965 when Elvis was filming 'Paradise, Hawaiian Style' - one of the many films he was contracted to make by his controlling manager Colonel Tom Parker.

Presley became very close to Jones while the latter was starring in Vegas. Night after night, Elvis would turn up to watch Tom perform and often join him on stage. Sometimes Jones did not seem to appreciate it and was heard to tell his road manager: "Hide the spare microphone - Presley's in."

A further indication that Elvis was fixated came when he sang to the Welshman while Tom was in the shower naked by leaning over the cubicle door in the star's changing room!

Following Presley's death on August 16, 1977, at the age of 42, apparently mainly from a heart attack, Jones paid a warm tribute to him. He said: "We were friends until just before he died. He had come to see me at The Flamingo in '68 because he said he wanted to make a stage comeback after not singing live for some years, and he felt I was the closest thing to him. I was one of the few solo singers performing in Vegas so he wanted to see how I went down.

"It gave him more confidence to make a comeback, which proved a huge success.

"We would talk about music...and jam through the night.

"I look back with great fondness and admiration for a great man and a remarkable singer."*

Before his decline, Presley was the best singer in the world, and his good looks were the envy of everyone in show business. It was tragic that towards the end of his life he became obese and suffered chronic constipation which it is believed contributed to a fatal heart attack in his bathroom, though the over-use of prescription drugs probably played a part. Unfortunately, many people now remember him in his bloated state.

To make matters worse, Elvis's reputation has been tainted by claims concerning teenage girls. Some are said to have performed for him by mud wrestling in white cotton panties and others, in similar attire, allegedly spent time with him in his bedroom.

Of course, his wife-to-be Priscilla Beaulieu was just 14 - ten years his junior - when they met in September 1959.

Elvis's sex secrets were disclosed in the book 'Elvis Presley: A Southern Life', by Joel Williamson, published by Oxford University Press. It claimed that the King of Rock 'n' Roll taught Priscilla how to make love in various ways short of full intercourse.

Priscilla said they didn't consummate their relationship until after they were married even though they lived together for six years until then.

It was claimed that Elvis, whose relationships seemed to be influenced greatly by the way his over-protective mother Gladys brought him up, did not have full sex with several of those he bedded, including an 18-year-old Natalie Wood when he was 21.

With so many females offering themselves, Presley, like Ali and Best, had temptation continually thrust in front of him.

British singer and actress Petula Clark was one of those who turned him down! She recalled in an interview with Elle Hunt in the Guardian that Elvis wanted a threesome when she and Karen Carpenter met him in his dressing room after a show in the early Seventies.

Petula said: "He was raring to go. Karen was lovely, but she was kind of innocent. I felt sort of responsible for her, so I got her out of there. Then I looked round, and Elvis was at the door, and he looked at me, like: 'I'm going to get you one day.' But he never did. I didn't find him that attractive."

Various disturbing stories and Elvis's sad decline, both mentally and physically, were bitter blows for his countless fans.

In contrast, another American icon, Marilyn Monroe, who was just 36 when she was found dead on August 5,

1962, was still glamorous and is thought of as having been one of the most desirable women in the world.

Marilyn died of an overdose from barbiturates, but it is still a mystery as to whether she took her own life, either intentionally or by accident, or she was murdered.

She is renowned for her renditions of the songs 'Happy Birthday' and 'I Wanna Be Loved By You'- and she sang the latter to me while sitting seductively on my lap! Unfortunately, the Marilyn I refer to was a gorgeous look-alike doing a tribute act in Bexhill-on-Sea!

I never got to meet the real Monroe or Diana Dors, whose picture I plastered on my bedroom wall as a teenager, but I contented myself with meeting various other lovely actresses and singers plus the world's greatest boxer of all time, Muhammad Ali, and playing football with the legendary George Best and Bobby Moore.

Another highlight was getting to perform with one of my favourite comedians, Jimmy Carr, who called me up on stage to take part in a sketch as part of his show in the Edinburgh Festival.

I was required to collapse dramatically and, upon doing so, was berated by Jimmy for my pathetic acting attempt. But, thinking that attack was the best form of defence, I decided to engage in a verbal battle with the man who is famous for his offensive 'put downs'.

I got carried away and told him that the water bottle he was drinking from was the nearest he was going to get to a Perrier, the award that comedians craved at the Edinburgh

Festival. Exchanging insults with the quick-witted Carr was taking a big risk, but he liked my joke and let me off lightly.

* There's a lot more about Tom Jones and memories of Elvis Presley in Over the Top and Back: The Autobiography by Tom Jones and in talks on www.elvis.com.au - Elvis articles, Elvis interviews and Elvis news by David Adams.

CHAPTER ELEVEN

Terry Scott was so demanding

Actors, cast as popular characters in television roles, are not always so lovable in real life.

This could be said about Terry Scott, who starred with June Whitfield in hit television sitcom 'Terry and June'.

In real life June Whitfield was equally as wonderful as the doting wife she played on screen.

But her screen husband Mr. Scott was apparently not so gracious.

The popular Daniel Hill, who appeared in one episode of 'Terry and June' when not involved in his own hit 'Waiting for God', recalled how Scott was rude to a fellow actor during filming.

Daniel said: "Terry was critical of this actor and rebuked: 'Is that how you're going to do it?' Even when the poor fellow asked for a bit of understanding because he had not worked for some time, he got little sympathy from Scott."

So Daniel, normally one of the kindest guys you could hope to meet, decided to teach Terry a lesson. He asked Scott if he would show him how to say his own lines, then requested him to do it twice more to wind him up! The script required Hill to berate Scott's character and when he finally delivered the lines himself he gave Scott a real roasting with a word-perfect, aggressive ticking off.

Hill revealed: "I was in a car with June coming back from location and I asked her: 'How do you put up with him?' She told me that she owed Terry a lot for helping her to become an established television star and that they worked well together. As she said, comics are sometimes a different breed."

The talented Hill, who also played June's son in 'Kingdom', which starred Stephen Fry, added: "June was the best - so professional. She knew everyone's lines as well as her own."

When I spoke to June Whitfield a few years ago she agreed that Terry Scott probably scared the daylights out of some people.

June told me: "Terry could be very critical, and his approach to other people was not always the best. He was a perfectionist and expected high standards from others. If actors didn't know their lines or were not on the ball then he got a bit annoyed. So there were a lot of people he did not get on with.

"But if I felt Terry was being too dominant I gave as good as I got and stood up for myself. I remember him telling me that I should play a scene a certain way so I said 'OK' and then did it the same as before. He was happy and told me that was better!"

However, June pointed out that Terry was a loving family man and had several good points. She said: "There were times when he was sweet, affable and charming. We worked so well together and I remember him with affection.

"In fact, people used to think we were not only married in 'Terry and June' but in real life as well."

June and Terry first appeared together in his TV series 'Scott On'. She recalled: "The producer and Terry were looking for someone to appear with him in a domestic sketch. I was very nervous when I met him as he was a well-established star, but he revealed that he had been nervous, too, and he told the producer 'She'll do'.

"It was the start of what proved to be a long television partnership and we struck up a very good rapport together."

Dame June died on December 28, 2018, after entertaining us for seven decades. She was both a great actress and a wonderful person who always put other people first.

This was the case in most of her films and sitcoms in which she made big name stars and comedians look good with her generosity and perfect timing. She played so many supporting roles that even her autobiography was called 'And June Whitfield'.

The delightful June recommended two of my books and was simply the kindest actress I ever came across. This was endorsed by Julia Sawalha, who played her granddaughter Saffron in the 'Absolutely Fabulous' series.

Following June's death, Julia posted: "Thank you #damejunewhitfield for teaching me my craft with such grace and dignity. I always wanted you to know how in awe of you I was, however, you were always far too humble to accept my adoration. You were a great source of inspiration to me. Bye-bye Gran."

CHAPTER TWELVE

Beatle Paul peed on rival's shoes

Husband-and-wife stars I've met include actors Brian Murphy and Linda Regan, Jeffrey Holland and Judy Buxton and Bachelors star Dec Cluskey and his wife Sandy, a former dancer in a host of shows.

The Bachelors were once one of the biggest singing groups in the world, out-selling the Beatles and the Rolling Stones in both records and at venues.

Ironically, today many people under the age of 25 might not know about the group's two brothers Dec and Con. But in their heyday they were instantly recognisable.

I've had the great pleasure of socialising with Dec and Sandy Cluskey because they live near me in Eastbourne and he kindly helped to judge a writing competition held by Anderida Writers, of which I am president.

Actually, his judging did not do me any favours with my own entry!

The very busy Dec submitted his markings for the competition later than the other two judges, newspaper editor Keith Ridley and freelance editor jay Dixon. On the first two sets of marks, my entry would have been in line for first prize, with nine and eight out of ten respectively. It transpired that all I needed from Dec was a seven to win the competition outright or a six to tie for first place. But after deciding to plough his way through more than 30 entries in one day, he gave me a meagre four!

Nevertheless, I love him to bits and he is one of the most charismatic people I know, with a wonderfully friendly, cheerful personality.

I warmly welcomed him to the Anderida awards night and got on tremendously well with him and his charming wife Sandy, who appeared as a dancer with the likes of Morecambe and Wise and Bruce Forsyth.

She told me this very amusing story of how Dec and she went to see a young Forsyth at London nightspot Talk of the Town and were afterwards invited to his dressing room.

Sandy recalled: "When we went into Bruce's dressing room we found it packed with celebrities, including Sammy Davis Junior and Jimmy Tarbuck.

"Bruce spotted us and made his way through the throng of people to greet us. Dec's face lit up with his usual broad smile as he prepared to accept Bruce's greeting, but instead Bruce went straight up to me and said 'Hello Sandy, it's so great to see you again.' "

It was obviously a blow to her husband's ego.

Dec also told me a wonderful story about how he met Paul McCartney when The Bachelors were the biggest group in Britain and The Beatles were just starting to emerge as their main rivals.

He recalled: "The Bachelors were playing the Pavilion in Bournemouth, the huge theatre near the sea front, while a new band called The Beatles were appearing in the small cinema opposite.

"I had heard about the frenzy that accompanied them everywhere, but we had never met, even though we had the same tailor, Dougie Millings, the guy who designed, and made, their famous round collared suits. I remember seeing these suits hanging on the rail surrounding his shop in Soho, waiting to be picked up. Dougie asked: 'Have you ever seen anything so crazy? Some nuts from Liverpool have ordered them'.

"After we finished our rehearsal in the afternoon at The Pavilion I walked across the road to have a peek at what these guys were up to.

"I went in the stage door. All was quiet and dim - not a soul about. I needed the loo and slipped into the backstage John.

"I was contentedly enjoying that lovely feeling as all the Guinness is emptied out when the door opened. A guy came in and stood beside me to relieve himself as well.

"We did the looking up to the sky thing that all men do at a urinal...then, as one, we glanced at each other. He jumped, recognising me. I jumped, recognising him ... and yes, the famous Beatle Sir Paul peed all over my shoes! I've still got them... stains and all!"

Dec adds that George Harrison happened to have the same girlfriend as him. But adds with a grin: "That's a story for another book."

The generous Dec did me an enormous favour by introducing the film premiere of the comedy play I had written, 'Hacking It', when it was shown for the first time at the Winter Garden Theatre, Eastbourne, in January 2012.

I actually welcomed the audience and gave Dec a glowing introduction. My stage manner 'impressed' him so much that he promptly took me to the next meeting of Eastbourne Speakers Club to polish it up.

Perhaps to Dec's surprise I won an award on my first visit for the 'Best Topics Speaker of the Night', but he was not too far off the mark when he joked: "Your content was great, but your delivery was rubbish!"

After that Dec and his fellow Speakers Club members helped me to cut down on my 'ums' and 'ers' and stop referring so much to my notes.

Brian Murphy is instantly recognisable from his television roles in 'George and Mildred' and 'Last of the Summer Wine', while his wife Linda Regan starred in holiday camp sitcom 'Hi-De-Hi' as Yellow-coat April and is now a successful thriller writer.

When I met Brian and Linda in September 2011 we talked about how the drop-dead gorgeous actress had come to fall for an actor who rarely got cast in romantic roles.

She recalled: "We appeared together as husband and wife on stage in 'Wife Begins at Forty' in Eastbourne. It wasn't love at first sight and, when Brian asked me out a couple of times during the run, I turned him down, making the excuse that I didn't want to get involved with someone who I was working with.

"So I quite expected him to ask me out again when the show came to an end but he didn't.

"I missed him so I drove over to see him at a theatre in Stratford where he was rehearsing for a new play. I suggested Brian took me for a drink some time; he asked 'when?' and I said 'today'.

"We were married within a year and have since enjoyed nearly 20 years of happiness together."

Brian told me: "I thought Linda wasn't interested in me after she refused to go out with me so I didn't ask her again. But when she turned up out of the blue I realised I was in with a chance."

Jeffrey Holland, who appeared with Linda in 'Hi-De-Hi' as comedian Spike, became patron of Anderida Writers so I got to know him and his wife Judy Buxton quite well and, like Brian and Linda, and Dec and Sandy, are also a delightful couple.

They took the trouble to read - and praise - my script for 'Hacking It'. Jeffrey also kindly wrote a very complimentary review about my wife Heather's children's book 'Mousey Mousey and the Witches' Spells', while Judy did likewise with Heather's 'Giant Sticker Monster and Other Children's Stories'. They gave similar encouragement to other Anderida members, as have their successors as

Anderida patrons, bestselling authors Peter James and Tamara McKinley.

Jeffrey Holland and Judy Buxton renew old acquaintances

I asked Jeffrey to provide an anecdote for this book and he came up with the following gem: "When my son Sam was born back in 1976, I was happily ensconced in a national tour of the stage musical of 'Dad's Army', with almost all the original TV cast.

"I was playing Private Walker, the black market spiv, having been promoted from the chorus as the actor who took the part in the London run, John Bardon, couldn't do the tour. It was the proudest time of my career to date! I was a member of Captain Mainwaring's Platoon in the Home Guard!

"We were playing at the Richmond Theatre in July, during one of the hottest summers on record, and towards the end of the midweek matinee performance I was called to the phone at the stage door.

"Having just enough time to take the call before the big finale, I rushed downstairs to hear my mother-in-law's voice telling me that my wife had gone into labour! (This was my first wife, Eleanor, not my present wife, Judy).

"Apparently she had gone in for a routine antenatal check-up and was told that she was having contractions!

"Knowing that her obstetric history was not good and there were certainly some risks ahead, I asked the two boys who understudied the two parts I played in the show to cover for me that night. I dashed to the station to get a train to Coventry where we lived at that time.

"I got to Eleanor's bedside by 7pm and the baby wasn't born until 2.30am! There were a few problems as anticipated so it was as well that I was there to be with her.

"What I hadn't given any thought to, though, was the wrath of Captain Mainwaring, alias Arthur Lowe! My priority had been to be with my wife in a dangerous situation, and not 'the show must go on!'

"When I arrived back at the theatre the following evening, I found a note in my pigeon hole saying: 'Mr Lowe would like to see you in his dressing room.' Oh dear!

"Girding my loins, I made my way up to Arthur Lowe's dressing room and knocked politely on the door. 'Come in!' he called.

"So in I went. Arthur was sitting at his dressing table applying a little colour to his moustache. He didn't look at me! You see, being of the old school, he did believe that 'the show must go on!' 'You wanted to see me, Arthur?' I asked.

"He scolded: 'What you did yesterday was very unprofessional. Babies are born all the time! You should have been here for the show!'

"In a sense he was right, of course, but when I explained my reasons for leaving in such a hurry and the need for me to be there, he melted just a little, and I was sent on my way.

"Needless to say, the first flowers to arrive at the bedside the following day were from the Lowes!"

CHAPTER THIRTEEN

Naked truth about The Spice Girls

The Spice Girls have repeatedly hit the headlines, particularly Mel B in her attempt to take her own life during her turbulent marriage to Stephen Belafonte and the existence of videos of the couple's threesomes with another woman*.

But one thing I don't think has been covered in the Press is that the girls ran about hotels naked. This was brought to light by the delightful Emma Bunton when she appeared on 'Would I Lie to You'.

She told fellow panellists: "When The Spice Girls stayed in hotels we played a special game to test who was the bravest. We used to dare each other to run in the hallways naked. We were allowed sometimes to carry a flannel - so you could choose a part to cover.

"I remember once the girls made me go to the lift and wait for it to arrive. You were lucky if it opened and no one was there.

"We would go two at a time and the first one back, knocking on the door, was the winner." She revealed "It is TRUE!"

Thousands of column inches have been devoted to The Spice Girls' other activities. Geri Halliwell, now married to Red Bull Formula One boss Christian Horner, and Mel C (Melanie Chisholm), both enjoyed relationships with Robbie Williams, while the Press have written endlessly about Posh Spice Victoria's marriage to David Beckham.

Robbie Williams, promoting his book 'Reveal' on 'The Graham Norton Show' in December 2017, revealed that to try to fool the paparazzi he smuggled Geri Halliwell out of his flat in a Hold-All. He said: "I literally put her in a duffle bag and put her over my shoulder. I had the paparazzi all taking pictures and I'm like, 'Hi, guys!' I put her in the boot of her car."

* Mel B told in her autobiography 'Brutally Honest' how, in December 2014, she attempted to take her life by swallowing 200 aspirin the night before she was due to be on the judging panel in a live X Factor show.

Mel realised she was making a mistake and, after being taken to intensive care in hospital, called X-Factor supremo Simon Cowell. This led to her missing the semi-final, but she defied doctor's advice to appear on live TV for the final the following day.

'Brutally Honest', by Melanie Brown, with Louise Gannon, published by Quadrille, also detailed how she took up to six lines of cocaine a day to help prepare for filming The X Factor.

Mel, who just can't keep secrets, also claimed this year that she once had a fling with Geri Horner.

CHAPTER FOURTEEN

Philip Green might have pipped Alan Sugar for The Apprentice job

Sir Philip Green, who obtained a High Court injunction in a bid to prevent the media publishing allegations concerning racism and sexual behaviour towards employees which he denied, had come close to being offered the starring role in 'The Apprentice' instead of Lord Alan Sugar.

I heard this story following my time as Controller of Information at Sky Television, and Lord Sugar confirmed it in his autobiography 'Alan Sugar - What You See is What You Get', published by Macmillan.

Lord Sugar believed Jane Lush, the controller of entertainment commissioning at BBC2 at the time they were planning to launch the programme in 2004, was "pushing hard for Philip Green".

Sugar added that Green told him he had also been contacted about the show, but didn't have enough time to do it.

However, if the producers had pursued their interest in the former BHS chief, then who knows? And I wonder what would have happened had Green fronted the show?

My guess is that there would have been a parting of the ways, probably before the adverse publicity involving him in 2018.

It was in November 2018 that Simon Cowell let it be known he had persuaded the under-fire businessman to give up his five per cent stake in Cowell's entertainment company Syco. The 'goodbye deal' was said to be worth around £10million.

Lord Sugar has, in my view, done a much better job hosting The Apprentice than Donald Trump did with the American version.

Some of Trump's decisions on the TV show, like those he has since made as US President, were questionable.

I was particularly annoyed when he let the bitchy Joan Rivers get away with some awful remarks about a fellow contestant, poker player Annie Duke, on America's 'The Celebrity Apprentice' in 2009.

It seemed so unfair that Trump declared Rivers the winner over Duke. But the controversial comedienne raised a hell of a lot of money on the show for charity and, with Trump, money talks!

CHAPTER FIFTEEN

Olivier's cutting wit

My great friend Alan G. Baker, a highly respected theatre director, first made his name as a very young actor in the West End, starring as the 'Winslow Boy' at the Haymarket Theatre in the1950s.

He worked with Sir Laurence Olivier and told me amusing stories about him, Sir Ralph Richardson, Sir John Gielgud and Noel Coward.

Alan was treated to a slice of Olivier's cutting wit after his first nervous appearance before the great man as a new member of the Old Vic Theatre cast in 1958.

Baker, then aged 21, was taking a cigarette break during the first read through for Richard The Third.

He recalled: "I was smoking Guards at the time and Olivier crossed the green room to speak to me. He saw what I was smoking and pulled a packet of Oliviers, named after him, from his pocket. 'Why do you smoke those?' he asked.

'I get coupons with them', I stuttered in reply.

'Ah', he said. 'You get acting parts with these'."

Alan, who in more recent years has acted and directed in local theatre productions, mainly with the Seaford Little

Theatre, also told me a very amusing tale about Sir Ralph Richardson when he was on stage with him.

He said: "Richardson was quite elderly and on one occasion 'dried' completely. So he walked to the prompt corner because he could not hear properly the cue that was given.

"After listening to the prompt a couple of times, Richardson finally heard his line and walked to the footlights to tell the audience 'very useful chap that, you know'. He got a round of applause."

Actors Alan Baker (left) and Brian Capron (right) join authors Tamara McKinley and me at the launch of Triple Tease

Alan also told me a great story about Sir John Gielgud getting caught out by his forgetfulness.

He explained: "Gielgud was having a meal with an actor in a restaurant when another actor walked in. Sir John said 'There's that awful fellow .....' but because his memory was so bad he actually named the actor he was sitting with. Seeing the look on the face of his companion, Sir John realised he had insulted him, so he quickly added: "Not you, dear chap, another actor with the same name as you!"

Then there was the story of Noel Coward walking in Leicester Square when he saw a big billboard proclaiming 'Dirk Bogarde and Michael Redgrave 'The Sea Shall Not Have Them'. His alleged reaction was: 'I don't see why not - everyone else has.' Could he simply have been referring to the fact that fans fantasized about Bogarde and Redgrave so much?

My favourite story of Alan's concerns Dame Edith Evans and her visit to Harrods Store in Knightsbridge.

It should be remembered that when emphasising a point she would adopt a very high pitched voice, as she had done in 'The Importance of Being Ernest' by going up a few decibels to deliver her famous line "handbags!" causing the sound system to blow in rehearsals!

During the war Edith was told that Harrods had received a consignment of pineapples so she went into the store to buy one.

The girl in the fruit department told her it would cost ten shillings and six pence. Edith, feeling this was excessively expensive, repeated in the top range of her voice "Ten shillings and six pence - here is eleven shillings, I think I trod on a grape on the way in."

Alan Baker, who has also directed films, explained to me how the screen was kind to some actors and unkind to others.

He said: "The cameras loved Richard Burton and Elizabeth Taylor who had such well-balanced faces. But that brilliant actress Flora Robson did not come across well on screen and was better on stage from a distance. Close up shots of some actors and actresses could portray a face that only a mother would love or age them considerably.

"Gielgud was one of those who looked older on screen - the camera would put up to 20 years on him!"

Alan was the executive director of my comedy 'Hacking It', which was filmed by movie makers Alan Tutt and Harry Lederman, the former chairman of The Friends of Devonshire Park Theatre.

But, despite my best efforts to write him into the play, the exuberant Mr. Baker could not be persuaded to appear before the cameras, and instead devoted his time to coaxing actors from Seaford Little Theatre and Eastbourne Underground Group to play the off-the-wall characters I had dreamed up.

"It's best to concentrate on one job," he remarked.

CHAPTER SIXTEEN

I just didn't find Abi Titmuss sexy

The most disappointing sex symbol I've met has been Abi Titmuss.

Don't get me wrong. I found Abi to be very pleasant to talk to, with no 'side' to her and she is far from being a dumb blonde, but I was expecting a drop dead gorgeous sex-on-legs glamour puss and she did not quite live up to my preconceived notions of her.

Many men have had a 'thing' about Abi and probably drooled over pin-up pictures of the nurse-turned-actress who has teased and tantalized by showing off her 36D-28-34 figure in revealing lingerie, but, in casual clothes and without full make-up, she didn't strike me as THAT sexy.

However, we had a lovely chat in the bar of the Devonshire Park Theatre after she had appeared there in September 2010 in John Godber's 25th anniversary production of Up 'n' Under involving a woman fitness instructor training a bunch of misfits for a men's rugby league match (despite the title it wasn't the raunchy type of role some theatre-goers might have expected).

Ironically, my friend Colin Dudley, who clearly thought Abi was sexy, could not avoid staring at her rather ample boobs, even though they were well covered. And he went bright red when a female member of the group standing around her said: "You can give her a stroke if you want to."

Tony was more impressed with Abi Titmuss' mind

It was some seconds before my friend realised that the lady was referring to Abi's little dog, who had accompanied her to the theatre!

My previous visualization of Abi had resulted from the story of the home-made sex tape that was shot with her former boyfriend and TV presenter John Leslie. She loyally stood by Leslie when he set out to clear his name of rape allegations concerning TV presenter Ulrika Jonsson.

When I met Abi she was 35 years old and had made the transition from pin-up girl to serious actress, having won a Best West End Debut award for her performance as a prostitute in Arthur Miller's 'Two Way Mirror'. So she deserves full credit for that.

TV personality Carol Vorderman certainly lived up to my expectations when I bumped into her at a party held in honour of the late Malcolm Richards, my former editor at the Richmond and Twickenham Times.

Carol won the 'Rear of the Year' award in both 2011 and 2014, beating younger candidates like internet sensation Pippa Middleton.

Some journalists suggested that her bottom was too big to wear figure-hugging dresses, in which she sometimes goes commando. But, although Carol might not be the same shape as when I was introduced to her, I reckon that lots of women would love to look like her in their fifties.

It is remarkable that Carol has had only a little Botox done. The seemingly ageless beauty says her secret is plenty of exercise (she walks about seven miles a day and does circuit training). Taking HRT also helps the 5ft 6in, nine-and-a-half stone 58-year-old keep fit.

Another 'more mature' female celebrity who impressed me with her looks and charisma was American singer-actress Cher, who I encountered in unusual circumstances at London Docklands. I found her to be as staggeringly attractive and engaging in real life as on the screen.

I briefly met Cher when she made a personal appearance at an informal function held in the Docklands by St. Mungo's, a charity which provides help and facilities for the homeless and unemployed.

She found herself surrounded by a big group of homeless people in the reception area and offered words of encouragement by telling them: "If you really want something you can usually figure out how to make it happen."

Quick as a flash, one unshaven, rather scruffy bloke replied: "Does that include having dinner with you at your hotel tonight?"

Shirley Anne Field, Patsy Kensit and Erin Boag also lived up to my expectations of them, while my wife Heather was bowled over by Erin's dance partner Anton du Beke.

Anton du Beke and Erin Boag flash their charming smiles

When we chatted to him and Erin backstage the charming Anton took Heather's hand and kissed it twice. He then gave her kisses on both cheeks when we said our good-byes.

One 'glamour girl' I did not seek to meet was 'X Factor' judge Cheryl Tweedy (also named Cole and Fernandez-Versini).

I didn't like the way the opinionated Geordie and her money-conscious ex-husband, former Chelsea footballer Ashley Cole, came across in certain situations.

England's one-time left-back, nicknamed 'Cashley' by many fans, angered his old club Arsenal and their supporters over a clandestine meeting with London rivals Chelsea while he was still with the Gunners.

He got more bad Press over allegations that he cheated on his wife. Cheryl and Ashley were divorced in September 2010 after four years of marriage. The decree nisi was granted on the grounds of Ashley's admitted unreasonable behaviour.

Cheryl had also hit the headlines for the wrong reasons long before her marriage. The former Girls Aloud singer was found guilty of assaulting a Guildford nightclub toilet attendant in 2003.

The pop star was sentenced to complete 120 hours of unpaid community service and pay her victim £500 compensation as well as £3,000 for prosecution costs. The singer had denied attacking attendant Sophie Amogbokpa, claiming she only punched her in self-defence.

When Cheryl became a judge on TV talent show 'X Factor' some of her views and decisions didn't impress me.

I could not see the justice in Cheryl throwing out viewers' favourite singer Gamu Nhengu so that she could put through to the 2010 finals two less charming girls, Katie Waissel and Cher Lloyd, who fluffed the songs they sang at the mentor's house stage of the competition!

Thousands of fans protested, but Cheryl, given the chance to redeem the situation when told she could add a 'wild card' to her choices, promptly ignored the talented Zimbabwe teenager again!

Cheryl's career later went downhill, and she suffered further break-ups with Jean-Bernard Fernandez-Versini and Liam Payne.

Fortunately, I found her more engaging when expressing her views as a 'Captain' on BBC's 'The Greatest Dancer', and hopefully she has learned from her mistakes.

CHAPTER SEVENTEEN

Injury-hit Faith switched from dancer to singer

Teenage sensation Faith Tucker's dreams of becoming a top dancer were shattered by a knee injury, but she showed amazing powers of recovery to earn acclaim as the UK's most talented young operatic singer.

The then 17-year-old, who went on to wow audiences in Britain's Got Talent this year, told me: "I won several dance awards, including Lincolnshire's Street Dance competition in 2008 when I was seven.

"But I then snapped ligaments in my knee during a dance routine, and three operations failed to put it right. I was heart-broken because I had been appearing on stage as a dancer for ten years since the age of three. But it made me all the more determined to have a career in show business as a singer so I added opera to my extensive vocal range."

The amazing Nottingham youngster has also become a prolific composer and her piece for choir and organ 'Gloria' was performed for a special evensong at St. Georges Chapel, Windsor Castle.

Faith is determined to make opera more popular with the masses, particularly youngsters.

She explained: "Not many youngsters listen to opera or think it is cool. But when they see someone as young as me making an impact as a classical singer it will hopefully change their minds.

Chatting with singer Faith Tucker

"Susan Boyle and Paul Potts both made the break through - despite being regarded as old fashioned in style and appearance. But there is still a long way to go and someone trendy like me can win over a whole new generation."

Unfortunately, sixth former Faith, having sailed through the first round of Britain's Got Talent after singing 'Granada', went out in the semi-finals.

I feel she should have chosen a song better known to the majority of voting viewers than Italian number 'Sei Tu La Ragione'. But I believe she has the talent and the charm to still become a mega star.

CHAPTER EIGHTEEN

Dalglish rang me to have a rant

Bobby Moore was so loved that people would go out of their way to please him.

But Bobby was reluctant to ask any favours when he worked with me on Sunday Sport. And he did not call one in from Kenny Dalglish in order to help our chief sports writer Hugh Southern as Hugh sought unsuccessfully to get an interview with the Liverpool manager.

This was back in 1988 and we were putting together previews for that year's FA Cup final in which Wimbledon, rank outsiders at 33-1 before the third round in January, turned the form book upside down to reach the final against strongly fancied Liverpool.

I had already interviewed two of the Liverpool players, and passed that story on to our sister paper the Daily Star, so I decided that, for our own Sunday Sport previews, I would chat to some of the Wimbledon players, and Hugh should get some quotes from Liverpool boss Dalglish.

Hugh, skilled at coming up with good story lines, experienced some difficulty in getting hold of King Kenny, and at an office conference Editor Drew Robertson, whose predecessor Mike Gabbert had departed to become Editor of the Daily Star, wanted the interview done pronto!

Drew said Hugh should leave for Liverpool immediately and present himself at the training ground to ask to see Dalglish. I pointed out that there was little chance that Kenny would give Hugh a lengthy interview without prior arrangement, so Drew turned to Bobby Moore and asked his opinion.

To my surprise, Moore, reluctant to disagree with the Editor, said it was worth giving it a try - so Southern was dispatched forthwith.

He phoned me later from Liverpool to report that he had been to Anfield and was informed it was not possible for him to see Dalglish. I told him that he would need to stay overnight and try again the next day.

Hugh pointed out that he did not have sufficient money with him, or a credit card, to enable him to stay in the Holiday Inn or a similar hotel. It was left to me to explain that the type of low budget accommodation Drew Robertson had in mind for him would not cost him anywhere near as much as the Holiday Inn!

The next day the unfortunate Hugh was again on the phone, telling me he had been to the training ground pleading to see Dalglish, but again without success. He had been reduced to sleeping in his underwear the previous night and was now soaked to the skin so I told him to return.

Ironically, one day later Dalglish phoned the office, and Hugh answered the phone to him. He must have thought his prayers had been answered until the Liverpool manager told him in a stern voice that he wanted to speak to me.

Kenny was not phoning to give Hugh an interview, but to complain that the story I had previously written, quoting two of his players, had appeared in the Daily Star.

Dalglish was aggrieved because the Liverpool players' pool had not asked for a fee for the interviews as they knew Sunday Sport had a very small budget. They would presumably have insisted on a payment from the bigger, more wealthy Daily Star to swell the players' FA Cup kitty.

I was dumbfounded at the thought of the great Kenny Dalglish finding time to ring me to complain about the players' pool missing out on a few hundred pounds when he and his squad were earning countless thousands. But perhaps this was just another example of King Kenny sticking up for his players and looking after their interests.

The funny thing about Dalglish in those days was when he was asked any awkward questions by journalists he would often answer in a broad Scottish accent that I found hard to make out. But in his complaint to me he spoke so clearly I could understand every single word!

Bobby Moore thought the whole thing was greatly amusing, and I believe even Hugh saw the funny side after securing a telephone interview with Liverpool legend Tommy Smith on how the final would go.

Of course, Tommy and almost everyone else were wrong with their predictions, because, against all odds, little Wimbledon beat the mighty Merseysiders 1-0.

Talking about getting things wrong, I am not alone in feeling that, while Dalglish deserved great credit for reviving Liverpool in his second spell as their manager, he made mistakes when it comes to public relations, particularly in his handling of the Luis Suarez affair.

Dalglish surprised me by backing an inappropriate decision that his players wear T-shirts in support of Suarez and claiming that the provocative Uruguayan striker should not have been suspended for eight games by the FA for racially abusing Manchester United's Patrice Evra.

But then Kenny really shocked me with his reaction after Suarez marred his first start following his return by refusing to shake hands with Evra as the teams lined up for another match against United in February, 2012.

The Liverpool manager, interviewed on Sky TV after the explosive 2-1 defeat by United, said he'd been unaware that Suarez had snubbed Evra.

Sky reporter Geoff Shreeves informed him firmly, but politely, that Suarez had, in fact, refused to shake Evra's hand.

Shreeves was scowled at by the dour Scot, who told him: "I think you are bang out of order to blame Luis Suarez for anything that happened out there." Dalglish refused to even criticise his player's conduct.

It was in stark contrast to the reaction of United boss Sir Alex Ferguson, who called for Suarez to be booted out of Anfield.

Sir Alex raged: "I just could not believe it... That player should not be allowed to play for Liverpool again. It could have caused a riot."

It was not until a day later that Dalglish and Liverpool seemed to fully realise the damage this had done to the club. They were then anxious to correct what had been a public relations disaster.

Suarez issued a statement of apology at 14.16pm, followed by others from Liverpool chief executive Ian Ayre at 14.30pm and Dalglish at 15.30pm.

Dalglish's statement said: "Ian Ayre has made the club's position absolutely clear and it is right that Luis Suarez has now apologised for what happened at Old Trafford.

"To be honest, I was shocked to hear that the player had not shaken hands, having been told earlier in the week that he would do so.

"But, as Ian said earlier, all of us have a responsibility to represent this club in a fit and proper manner and that applies equally to me as Liverpool manager.

"When I went on TV after yesterday's game I hadn't seen what had happened, but I did not conduct myself in a way befitting of a Liverpool manager during that interview and I'd like to apologise for that."

Managers should learn that if they are dismissive of questions asked them by reporters, they are usually failing to give their own supporters the information they are seeking.

It's the same with politicians.

When successive party leaders David Cameron, Theresa May, Ed Miliband and Jeremy Corbyn have taken cheap shots at each other in the House of Commons, they have refused to provide sensible answers that us (the voters) want to know!

It would be great if politicians improved their knowledge of public perceptions and their manners at Prime Minister's Question Time!

One thing they could learn from King Kenny and many other past and present football managers is how to motivate and inspire their teams.

Dalglish rode his luck at times, as he did when Liverpool pipped gallant Cardiff 3-2 in a nerve-racking penalty shoot-out at the end of the Carling Cup final in February 2012 after being held to a 2-2 draw following extra-time.

But he deserved full credit for ending Liverpool's six-year wait for a trophy by fielding his strongest team in a competition which many other managers under-valued.

They have even done so in the FA Cup in recent years. Those managers who have gone out in early rounds after selecting teams full of reserves have surely been misguided. They presumably felt they were justified in saving their key players for the league games ahead, but they were passing up a chance of glory for everyone at their club.

Dalglish's former Scotland manager Tommy Docherty agrees. He told me: "I believe managers who don't field their strongest side are cheating their supporters and belittling the competition.

"It has backfired on them because if they had selected their best team in every round they might have made it to the final. Winning a cup competition would have been great to have on their CV and a real boost for their club."

Docherty also had high praise for Dalglish as a player. He said: "I gave him his first 15 caps for Scotland in the 1970s. Jock Stein, the former Scotland manager, told me I was wrong to pick Kenny because he wasn't ready, but he was the best player in our team - a different class to the rest."

CHAPTER NINETEEN

Peter Sellers made Britt squirm

When I interviewed actress Britt Ekland I found her to be guarded about what she would say, especially concerning her former husband Peter Sellers.

But she did not deny he was obsessive, and this applied to his relationship with members of the Royal family.

The former Hollywood actress, who probably had better things to do than be interviewed by me for her forthcoming appearance in a local theatre production, could not be coaxed into saying much more on the subject.

However, her revelation that: "I'd squirm with embarrassment at the lengths he (Sellers) would go to in order to ingratiate himself with the Royal family," speaks volumes.

In her autobiography 'True Britt' she revealed: "I was completely unaware of his connection with the British monarchy. One afternoon before we married he had disappeared, saying that he had to do something 'important'.

"I was to learn he had spent the afternoon having tea with the Queen Mother at Clarence House."

Sellers was a close friend of Princess Margaret and she appeared in one of his home movies.

Britt, who in her prime was one of the world's most beautiful women, told me she did not approve of the biopic about Sellers. She stressed: "It bore no relationship to real life whatsoever. Nobody bothered to ask me what life with Peter Sellers was like.

"I could have told them so much. I still have all my diaries, photos and letters Peter and I exchanged."

My 20 minute chat with Britt in 2005 was to preview her forthcoming appearance on stage in the comedy 'Just Desserts!' at Richmond Theatre - a long way from the height of her Hollywood career in which she starred in two films with Sellers before divorcing him and had appeared as a Bond girl in The Man with the Golden Gun in 1974..

But the stylish Swede insisted: "I don't miss the Hollywood lifestyle. I'm still leading a hectic life and work nine months of the year. I simply keep fit by walking my dog and doing stretches. The reason I still look good is down to genetics."

At the then age of 62, she was no doubt less under the publicity spotlight than in her heyday when her romances with Rod Stewart and Warren Beatty hit the headlines.

Britt, who described Beatty as "the most divine lover of all with a libido that was as lethal as high octane gas," told me that modern actors lacked the charisma of former Hollywood greats.

She said: "When I was at the height of my career in the 1960s, there were some real characters in Hollywood. Now actors lack charisma and stature leading - men like Tom Cruise are on the short side."

One of her career highlights was playing opposite Michael Caine in 'Get Carter'. Asked about the remake, she commented: "I haven't seen it and wouldn't want to. What makes Sylvester Stallone think that he has the sensitivity to do what Michael Caine did?

"Unfortunately, some of the giants of the screen can never be replaced."

But fellow actress Patsy Kensit disagreed. She insisted to me: "There are still some very big personalities around such as Hugh Grant and George Clooney."

My interview with Patsy at the Richmond Theatre underlines why it does not always pay for a journalist to be completely upfront or to underestimate the opposition.

Just before fellow journalist Catherine Usher and I did a joint interview with Miss Kensit for two local papers, Catherine showed me an article in a tabloid in which Patsy had talked openly about her love life.

But Catherine left it to me to ask Patsy to confirm that her first three husbands had been the true loves of her life. Patsy replied that she did not want to talk about her private life, which seemed slightly hypocritical seeing that she had told all to the national paper.

As a result of my tame and perfectly legitimate question, the Press Officer who was accompanying Patsy asked me to let her see my story before it was published in the Richmond and Twickenham Times Series so that she could have the right to approve it.

I refused, saying that Patsy had not been offended by the question in any way, as she had proved by posing for pictures with me and even running her hand across my chest to make the pictures look more intimate. But I said I would not include anything about her love life in my story.

The female Press Officer did not ask the innocent looking Catherine if she could see her story before it went into print. So she must have been shocked, as I was, when Cathy lifted Patsy's most revealing quotes from the tabloid paper exclusive, as well as from other cuttings, disclosing in her story extensive details about Miss Kensit's romances.

Even so, there have been other relationships which Cathy did not mention - those allegedly with Ally McCoist, Calum Best, David Walliams, Matt Holbrook, Jean-Christophe Novelli and beatboxer Killa Kela.

Patsy had turned to McCoist following her marriage break-up with Liam Gallagher, which had caused her to say: "I'm so happy that all the mess I used to have to deal with is not my mess anymore."

Unfortunately, there was a lot more mess in store for her.

Patsy did not deny she was having an affair with married footballer McCoist and when it was reported in the Press in September 2001 she may have felt this would cause him to leave his wife.

Instead, it came out that he had also been having an affair with 28-year-old air hostess Donna Gilbin. And to complete Kensit's embarrassment, McCoist promptly ended their relationship.

Patsy married for the fourth time on April 18, 2009 but she and DJ Jeremy Healy separated less than a year later in February 2010.

Kensit vowed never to wed again following this split, describing it as 'embarrassing and humiliating.'

Poor Patsy has had it tough most of her life. Her father was not the antiques dealer she'd been led to believe, but had gangland connections and a criminal record. James 'Jimmy The Dip' Kensit was an associate of the notorious London gangsters the Kray twins and the Richardsons and he served time in prison before she was born.

Goodness knows what that Press officer would have said if Cathy or I had brought any of this up at our interview!

Patsy, a gritty English girl from Hounslow, Middlesex, had starred with some of the biggest actors in the world, having played opposite Mel Gibson in 'Lethal Weapon 2' and Anthony Hopkins in 'A Chorus of Disapproval'. Yet she admitted to me that sharing the Richmond stage in 'Aladdin' with highly respected Shakespearean actor Simon Callow was rather daunting.

She said: "I was in awe of Simon and it took me ages to make eye contact with him."

As Patsy was performing in a low cut pantomime costume, it may have been equally hard for him to make eye contact with her! After all, she had a breast augmentation which took her bust measurement from a 32B to a 35C.

Another actress who made a big impression on me was Linda Gray, the star of TV soap opera 'Dallas'.

We had a most enjoyable chat after one of her stage performances and I found her to be most friendly.

Linda revealed that originally she was given only a small part in the first series of 'Dallas', which was to become one of the most successful ever soaps.

She said: "Larry Hagman and I were so wonderfully evil together, and had so much fun acting off each other, that they beefed up my part.

"In the first episode I wasn't referred to and never as J.R.'s wife." But she loved playing Sue Ellen and told me: "A lot of women could relate to her."

CHAPTER TWENTY

Age has caught up with Petula

Age eventually catches up with all of us including even the most glamorous of stars.

Classic examples of this are singers Mick Jagger, Tommy Steele and Petula Clark.

When I reviewed one of Petula's stage shows a few years ago she looked as lively and bouncy as ever on stage.

But in my interview with her afterwards I was shocked to see that the ageing process had caught up with her. Fortunately she had lost none of her charm and sparkle.

The singer, actress and composer, who was born on November 15th, 1932, has had an amazing career spanning eight decades during which she has sold more than 68 million records!

She revealed: "At first I didn't want to be a singer, but for a youngster in England during the war there wasn't an awful lot around."

Her father had taken her to see Flora Robson on stage back in 1938 and she originally set her mind on becoming an actress. She said: "I wanted to be Ingrid Bergman more than anything else in the world."

Petula Clark accepts youngsters don't know who she is

I found Petula to be totally realistic when she told me: "Maybe many youngsters don't know who I am because most of them are so engrossed in the current pop scene. I don't find that frustrating, just somewhat amusing.

"The world is constantly changing and longevity cannot be guaranteed. Perhaps Madonna will be the last big star to survive the test of time."

Even those youngsters to whom the name Petula Clark means nothing should recognise Downtown, her smash hit record which topped the US charts and launched her American career over 55 years ago.

Some stars still look remarkably good for their age such as Joan Collins, Cliff Richard, Shirley Bassey and Tony Blackburn.

Tony, the winner of the ITV reality programme 'I'm A Celebrity...Get Me Out of Here!' in 2002, was the first disco jockey to broadcast on BBC Radio 1 in 1967.

You would think that a DJ, who had as much success and made as many radio and television appearances as Blackburn did in those days, would be full of confidence, perhaps even slightly arrogant.

But that was not the case. He actually seemed to be the opposite when I rescued him from queueing outside Stringfellows night club where Sunday Sport were holding a celebration party in the late 1980s.

And Tony even did a runner some 10 years earlier when my friend Clive Hogben yelled out to him in the street because he had left his wallet in Clive's shop.

Clive recalls: "Tony Blackburn came into the shop where I was assistant manager to order a music centre.

"After he had gone I saw that he'd left his wallet behind so I ran out of the shop after him and shouted his name. He did not recognise me, and seeing me running towards him clearly frightened him.

"So Tony ran off down Tottenham Court Road with me in pursuit. I grabbed him outside the underground station, and he was a very relieved man when I explained that I simply wanted to return his wallet."

CHAPTER TWENTY-ONE

Frankie Howerd hid fact he was gay

I have met many comedians, including those unique greats Max Miller, Frankie Howerd, Pub Landlord Al Murray, Jimmy Carr, Cannon and Ball, Joe Pasquale and Jim Tavaré.

Tony with Paul Tonkinson and Frank Skinner

Jim gave me backstage access to a charity event he held so that my son James and I could chat briefly to him and more of Britain's top funny men Tim Vine, Lee Mack, Harry Hill, Paul Tonkinson and Frank Skinner.

Doing stand-up can be one of the toughest jobs in show business as I discovered when I tried it myself.

I got the laughs with a Bob Monkhouse-style routine containing loads of wife jokes, but I was terrified I would dry up. And even when I got a standing ovation from a crowd of 1,000-plus, I didn't have to worry about television ratings like real comedians do. The prospect used to worry Frankie Howerd so much he was often physically ill with stage fright before a performance.

It may surprise many people to learn that the slick, super confident Al Murray*, who has superb rapport with his audiences, found it difficult to cope with a heckler at one time.

Soon after he created his know-it-all persona of the 'Pub Landlord' I saw Al perform in the White Hart Hotel in Kingston, Surrey. Everything went well until a heckler persisted and Al cut short his performance after trying, without success, to explain that he was simply playing a character.

So how did he turn the tables and become such an expert at ribbing audiences? Al, told me: "By gaining experience and being sheer bloody-minded."

Tim Vine*, the master of one-liners and puns, confirms: "You have to believe in yourself - and keep coming up with new ideas and material."

Tim has twice won the prize for the funniest joke of the Edinburgh Fringe Festival. In 2010 it was "I've just been on a once-in-a-lifetime holiday. I'll tell you what, never again."

In 2014, he came up with another gem: "I decided to sell my Hoover....well it was just collecting dust."

The worst thing for comedians is when television networks turn their backs on them. Razor-sharp jokesters Tommy Cannon and Bobby Ball told me how tough it had been to be largely ignored by TV until they bounced back by appearing on the reality show 'I'm A Celebrity...Get Me Out Of Here' in 2005.

They continued to wow audiences, including those in the States when in 2018 they starred in ITV's 'Last Laugh in Vegas', together with other popular veteran British entertainers, among them the 'never-ageing' Anita Harris.

Cannon and Ball's performances with Johnnie Casson and Stu Francis were also hilarious in The Dressing Room, written by Bobby, and combining sitcom with variety and comedy.

Tommy and Bobby* had a big fall out during their heydays in the 1980s, but then got very close again and became Christians.

Bobby commented: "It may have been egos. I thought I was the main one in the act and Tommy thought he was the main one in the act." He paused for effect before joking: "He should have realised it was me."

A similar thing happened to Little and Large[*], which was one of the topics of conversation when I interviewed Syd Little in 2011.

Eddie Large had revealed in an interview the previous year that he hadn't spoken to Syd for ages.

Syd claimed: "We would both think up sketches and I used to get frustrated because mine weren't accepted...And I felt bullied."

But Eddie, the star of the act in which Syd played the straight man, disagreed. He said: "That's not how I remember it."

What brought the act to a sudden end was Eddie's heart problems. He recalled: "I had to stop working and have a heart transplant."

David Walliams and Matt Lucas, who enjoyed a worldwide smash hit comedy with Little Britain, had a seven-year 'feud'. In the book, 'Little Me', Matt revealed they were "often at loggerheads" and in one row they exchanged insults.

Now they have resumed their friendship and Walliams told the Sun newspaper in June this year: "We hope to do something together in the near future, but there is no immediate plan."

The multi-talented David, who has been a judge on Britain's Got Talent for eight seasons and sold more than 32 million children's books, stressed that nothing beats being a Dad. He explained: "It is the best thing of all and totally life-changing. You feel there is finally some meaning to your life."

Walliams revealed in his autobiography that he had gay experiences during his youth, but, as an adult, he has enjoyed relationships with several high profile women, including the late Caroline Aherne - a secret liaison - Patsy Kensit, Geri Halliwell and model Lauren Budd when she was 18 and he was 37. He married another model, Lara Stone, but they split up after five years.

Most comedians have had dips in their careers, as was the case with Frankie Howerd, who was haunted for many years by the fear that his fans would discover he was gay. He even paid blackmail demands to conceal it.

Frankie was also paranoid about his hair loss, but when I met him in his dressing room it was obvious he was wearing a wig and there seemed to be a trace of glue at the top of his sideburns.

I found him to be in a good mood and very friendly but fortunately not over-friendly, as he apparently was on one occasion when he was alone with Bob Monkhouse, who quickly made his excuses and left!

At the time I met him, the so camp Frankie was making a comeback after his career had taken a dive. He was greatly relieved to be able to bounce back due to new satirical material written for him by Ray Galton and Alan Simpson.

Ray Galton and Alan Simpson came to tea

Galton and Simpson gave me some useful tips when they came round to tea with my wife Heather and I at our house in Twickenham after I had met Alan on various occasions and interviewed Ray. They also told me about the sad demise and suicide of one of Britain's greatest comedians, Tony Hancock, who felt so insecure he was seldom satisfied in either his professional or private life and resorted to drink.

Hancock committed suicide on June 25th, 1968 at the age of 44. And Ray Simpson said: "I was not shocked when I was told about it. I had expected it for years - it was the only way out for him."

Galton and Simpson compared the careers of old time comedians with the likes of Bruce Forsyth and Jimmy Tarbuck, who became overnight successes by hosting 'Sunday Night At The London Palladium'.

It was back in 1958 when Forsyth was appearing at the Royal Hippodrome in Eastbourne that impresario Val Parnell booked him to compère 'Sunday Night at the

Palladium'. But Bruce showed no gratitude to the Hippodrome. He recalled in the television programme '100 Years of the Palladium', "I got the call from Val when I was working in this terrible theatre at Eastbourne with a cast of 10 and an orchestra of two pianos and drums. I went from that to a 30-piece orchestra as host at the Palladium, the biggest job on television."

The outspoken entertainer possessed many endearing qualities, but admitted he had an ego. Other comedians used to tell jokes about it. My favourite was when Bruce supposedly made a personal appearance at an old people's home. He was in the reception area when an old person asked if she could help him.

Forsyth allegedly replied: "Do you know who I am?" And the old person said: "Ask matron, she'll tell you."

Brucie claimed he changed a lot over the years. He told Jenny Johnston in an interview published in the Daily Mail's Weekend magazine in January, 2012: "I'm quite shocked myself when I listen to what I sounded like 30 years ago. The pitch is completely different now - everything is much deeper.

"It was a bit camp, wasn't it?...People did think I was gay when I first started...I proved afterwards that I wasn't gay - probably too much in some regards."

Bruce became a TV legend, of course, and few would begrudge him finally receiving in October, 2011, at the ripe old age of 83, the knighthood he had waited for so long after 70 years in show business.

Talking of legends, Max Miller was Britain's top variety hall comic in the 1930s through to the 1950s and I met him in his last West End show at the Palace Theatre in 1959.

I was just 16 when my grandfather Reg and stepfather George treated me to a night out to see The Cheeky Chappie, famous for his flamboyant suits and risqué rapid-fire jokes that often got him into trouble with the censors.

Apparently, Max was less quick to part with his money. This probably accounted for the fact that, after we found him in the bar at the interval and bought him a drink, he did not turn up afterwards to return the favour as he had promised.

Fellow comedian Roy Hudd, the president of the Max Miller Appreciation Society, later revealed that the thrifty Max was not in the habit of buying drinks for others! But, like Tommy Cooper, he was more generous with his time and in spreading happiness to millions.

Max used to say "There'll never be another" - yet variety king Roy Hudd has given great impersonations of him on stage and TV to remind us of what we are missing.

* Al Murray has written several books including 'The Pub Landlord's Great British Pub Quiz Book', 'Al Murray: The Pub Landlord's Book of British Common Sense', 'Let's re-Great Britain' and 'Al Murray The Pub Landlord Says Think Yourself British', while Tim Vine has written 'The Biggest Ever Tim Vine Joke Book', The (Not Quite) Biggest Ever Tim Vine Joke Book'

and 'The Tim Vine Bumper Book of Silliness: Daft Jokes, Crazy Pictures, Utter Nonsense'.

* It's also worth checking out Larger than Life: My Autobiography by Eddie Large, with Stafford Hildred, and 'Little by Little' by Syd Little, while Cannon and Ball have brought out books and DVDs.

CHAPTER TWENTY-TWO

Pasquale's talent show votes secret

I had to make do with a telephone interview with comedian Joe Pasquale, but it was an enjoyable experience because he was prepared to answer most of my questions fully and frankly.

One thing he did not talk so freely about was his attempt to swing the voting in his favour while appearing as an unknown on television talent show New Faces in 1987.

His high-pitched voice seemed to go even higher as he admitted that a little help from several hundred new 'friends' put him on the way to stardom.

Joe later made a 'full confession' when appearing on ITV's 'The Talent Show Story' - 25 years after the event.

He said: "Before I went on 'New Faces' I was a bingo caller and refereed wrestling at a holiday camp, so I had nothing to lose.

"One of the judges was Ken Dodd and he gave me advice on how to improve my act. I did what he said and won the heat.

"I then needed to win the postcard vote to reach the final. I was still working at a holiday camp where we had about 400 people staying each week. I bought a job lot of 5,000 postcards and dished them out to guests after I had filled them in. All they had to do was stick a stamp on and post them."

Joe gave a sly grin as he added: "Whether they sent them in I don't know, but I got through on the viewers' votes."

Having a laugh with Joe Pasquale

In the final, decided by votes being phoned in across the country, Joe was pipped by ventriloquist Jimmy Tamley. They were level on points when the last telephone vote from the Midlands gave Tamley victory.

But Pasquale recalled: "The fact I came second meant I got a wave of sympathy, saying 'you should have won'. I'd rather have 'you were robbed' than people going 'how did you win?'

Joe, who I later met when he appeared in Eastbourne, may act the fool with a succession of visual gags on stage, but he is one shrewd cookie. He proved this by increasing his popularity through appearing on, and winning, 'I'm A Celebrity...Get Me Out Of Here!' in 2004.

Talking of visual humour, three of the greatest natural comedians have been Tommy Cooper, Norman Wisdom and Ken Dodd. That view was endorsed by fellow entertainer Chris Stone, a vice president of Clowns International.

He told me: "Norman Wisdom and Ken Dodd were also vice presidents of Clowns International, which has 300 working clowns as members, and both of them appeared at our festivals.

"When Ken came to our festival in Bognor in 1989 it was his first public appearance after being charged with tax evasion in a court case that lasted three weeks and resulted in him being acquitted.

"We went through the town on an open top bus and Ken was worried about the reception he would get from the public. He told us he feared some of the crowd might boo him. But 100,000 people cheered their heads off as he waved to them - they loved the fact he had got the better of the Inland Revenue."

To rub it in to the tax man, Ken joked: "I told the Inland Revenue I didn't owe them a penny because I lived near the seaside."

Two days before his death at the age of 90 in March, 2018, Sir Ken married his long-time love Anne Jones. This meant she inherited his £27.5million fortune - and prevented the taxman taking £11m from the estate.

Chris added: "Ken and Norman Wisdom have been two of the greatest comics I've come across. They, like Tommy Cooper, were blessed with the ability to make people laugh before they even opened their mouths.

"Norman was also a great prankster. I remember when he was due to appear at a Clowns International event in Southport. He came into the Green Room before the show limping and said he wouldn't be able to go on as he was feeling ill.

"We were all very concerned about him as he sat there looking poorly. After all, he was about 70 years old at the time. Then suddenly he leapt up, did a forward roll and said 'I'm OK now'. He went on to give a hilarious performance."

CHAPTER TWENTY-THREE

United could have ended up with Venables

Apart from Bobby Charlton, I also interviewed a lot of other Manchester United icons, including Pat Crerand, Lou Macari and Gordon McQueen, particularly during my time as Sports Editor of Fleet Street News Agency, which provided stories to all the national papers.

My chats with United manager Sir Alex Ferguson, club chairman Martin Edwards and other insiders at Old Trafford resulted in some very interesting revelations.

This included the fact that United came close to appointing an outspoken, love-him-or-'hate'-him Cockney as their manager in Terry Venables.

When Martin Edwards and his fellow directors Charlton, Maurice Watkins and Mike Edelson appointed Ferguson back in November 1986, as a replacement for Ron Atkinson, they also seriously considered Venables for the job.

They were impressed by the fact El Tel had taken Barcelona to the European Cup final that year and had won the Spanish League the previous season.

But Ferguson's great record with Aberdeen made him the No. 1 choice, and only if he had turned United down would Venables have got the job.

Unfortunately, this information was given to me 'off the record' which was a pain in the neck because it meant I was honour bound not to use the name of my source or what they said.

During his amazing 26 years in charge of United, Alex Ferguson proved to be one of the greatest managers ever by winning 38 trophies, including 13 Premier League titles, five FA Cups and two UEFA Champions League titles.

Some journalists might also tell you he was among the most intimidating, depending what sort of mood he was in when they encountered him!

It's as if there were TWO Alex Fergusons. Sometimes he could appear to be a bit of a 'smart Alec' - confrontational, critical and sarcastic. On other occasions he was very caring, accommodating and compassionate.

I was fortunate to talk to him two or three times on the phone when he was still finding his feet at Old Trafford back in 1986, and found him to be helpful and informative, which was very good of him, especially as we'd never met.

To me Sir Alex Ferguson, CBE, is a true legend. But I expect Sir Alex would have been less friendly towards me had we met after my comments about him when I made one of my regular appearances as a sports analyst as part of BBC television's News 24 in February 2003.

He had injured his own star player David Beckham by angrily kicking a boot across the dressing room, causing it to hit Beckham just above the left eye.

The incident occurred when Ferguson showed his displeasure at losing 2-0 to old rivals Arsenal in the fifth round of the FA Cup.

I was asked what I thought about Ferguson's reaction. I acknowledged that it was an accident, but made it clear that I felt Fergie was out of order in kicking a boot about, and should learn to curb his temper.

Ferguson laughed it off. He said: "It was a freakish incident. If I tried it 100 or a million times it couldn't happen again. If I could do it again I would have carried on playing!"

Some United players deserved to receive Fergie's 'hair-dryer' rollickings far more than Beckham.

Dwight Yorke upset his manager on several occasions, but probably none more so than when he and the then Aston Villa goalkeeper Mark Bosnich were found to have taken part in a romp with four girls.

Yorke secretly videoed the drink-fuelled sexual activities at his luxury house in Sutton Coldfield. The video showed him and Bosnich giving thumbs-ups to the secret camera and wearing women's clothing as a joke.

They would have got away with it had Yorke not thrown the video out in his rubbish bin. Unfortunately for him a 'Sun reader' found it - and when the pictures appeared in print Fergie was understandably furious.

Even a disciplinarian like Ferguson was not able to prevent other United players being involved in kiss-and-tell encounters.

Among the most damaging were the revelations about Ryan Giggs, who was named in Parliament as the footballer who had taken out an injunction to avoid claims of an affair with Big Brother's Imogen Thomas becoming public.

Giggs was understood to have spent around £200,000 on legal fees trying to keep a lid on the affair.

Ironically, it also came to light that he had an eight-year relationship with his sister-in-law Natasha Giggs.

There was massive Press coverage about it as the 29-year-old Natasha said she was a 'fool' to risk her marriage to the player's brother Rhodri for the thrill of having a relationship with someone as famous and admired as the then 38-year-old star.

The 'off-the-record' revelation about Terry Venables being the second choice to Fergie for the United job reminds me of an amusing story when I was Sports Editor of the Lancashire Evening Telegraph and Star in Blackburn at the start of the Eighties.

My main two sports writers Peter White and Keith McNee provided most of our page leads, but we also had an excellent writer in former Northern Ireland international soccer star Jimmy McIlroy, who had been possibly the greatest player Burnley ever had.

On one occasion Jimmy came up with the best story of the day following his interview with then Blackburn Rovers manager Howard Kendall, and so I told one of my sub-editors to use it as the back page lead.

After a few minutes the sub-editor came up to me and said: "Tony, have you read much of this story?"

"Only the first three paragraphs," I replied. He directed my attention to the fourth paragraph in which McIlroy quoted Kendall as saying: "Completely off the record..."

Jimmy had not appreciated what 'off the record' meant and was disappointed when I told him we were having to ditch his 'exclusive' because Kendall was giving the information only on a 'not-for-publication' basis.

CHAPTER TWENTY-FOUR

Matthews hauled up over spending six pence

Two of the most charming male personalities I've interviewed were old time footballers Sir Stanley Matthews and Sir Tom Finney.

They were almost certainly the greatest players of their generation and yet they were so natural and modest.

Steven Gerrard, Dave Mackay and Frank McLintock, with Tony looking on

Few multi-millionaire footballers have shown a similar degree of modesty, with the notable exceptions of former Chelsea hero Frank Lampard and Liverpool legend Steve Gerrard, both of whom I also found charming to interview.

Ironically, Matthews was rated more highly than any of the current stars by his adoring Blackpool fans. Yet he was not given the respect due to him by some of his 'masters' at the Football Association.

I remember Matthews saying that when he travelled to Scotland to play for England at Hampden Park in April, 1948 he changed trains at Carlisle where he bought a cup of tea and a scone for six pence in the station buffet.

He submitted an expense claim for this to the FA and had it rejected by some petty accounts person!

Here was England's top star, who had helped to attract a massive crowd of more than 130,000 to Hampden Park and earn England a 2-0 victory, being scolded over charging expenses of less than £1 in present day values for a cup of tea.

Can you imagine what would happen if the FA did that to one of today's over-paid players?

Matthews' match fee for helping England beat the Scots was a meagre £14, and he had to travel from Stoke to Glasgow on a second-class rail ticket.

Matthews played his final game at the ripe old age of 50 for Stoke City on February 6th, 1965 after seeing out his career on the maximum wage of £20 a week!

The Wizard of Dribble scored 71 goals in 701 league and cup games, but he will always be remembered for his role in helping Blackpool come back from 3-1 down to beat Bolton 4-3 in the 1953 FA Cup final.

Stanley Mortensen scored a hat-trick in that Wembley epic, yet it has always been known as 'The Matthews final.'

I played with Mortensen and some of the other Blackpool players from that team in a charity match years later while on holiday at the seaside town.

When I was brought on as a substitute, the match commentator, comedian Freddie 'Parrot Face' Davies, took one look at my bulky frame and announced: "Now, taking the field wearing two pair of shorts, is Tony Flood."

I found that Mortensen was unassuming, and was not at all bitter that a final in which he scored three goals should be named after someone else!

Matthews was given a free role in the Blackpool side, mainly due to his tremendous skill and partly because manager Joe Smith was not a great one for tactics.

Sir Stanley revealed: "Joe just told us to go out and enjoy ourselves.

"At half-time against Bolton we were losing 2-1, but we remained calm. We simply sipped our tea and listened to Joe. He didn't rant or rave - he just told us to keep playing our normal game."

After Mortensen had levelled the scores, Matthews set up the winner for Bill Perry in the last minute of injury time. He recalled in 'The Way It Was: My Autobiography': "Ernie Taylor rounded Langton and found me wide on the right. I took off for what I knew would be one final run to the by-line.

"I jinked past Banks and, as Barrass came in, I pulled the ball back to where experience told me Morty would be. In making the cross I slipped on the greasy turf and, as I fell, my heart and hopes fell also.

"I saw that Morty was not where I expected him to be, but had peeled away to the far post. For five years we'd had this understanding. He knew exactly where I'd put the ball. Now, in this game of all games, he wasn't there.

"But Bill Perry raced up from a deep position and coolly stroked the ball wide of Hanson and Ball on the goal-line into the corner of the net."

Matthews was never booked in almost 700 league games spanning 39 years. No modern day player will ever match that record!

CHAPTER TWENTY-FIVE

Osgood feared for Ted Drake

Perhaps the most fun I had was running a soccer coaching course for youngsters with former Chelsea star Peter Osgood in Tolworth, Surrey.

I organised the course through a local newspaper and it attracted almost 150 young applicants, including my own son James, a rather reluctant recruit as soccer did not really appeal to him.

Osgood and another former Chelsea player, Allan Harris, agreed to take the coaching, and I invited along soccer legend Ted Drake to make a special guest appearance.

Drake had set a club record as a centre-forward with Arsenal by scoring 44 league and cup goals in the 1934-5 season and went on to manage Chelsea, leading them to their first ever championship in 1954-55.

This had happened before the youngsters on our course were born so, of course, they didn't know who it was when they saw this well-built elderly man stride over to where we were coaching in groups.

Despite the fact it was raining, Ted was wearing a smart blazer and grey trousers.

One of the kids in my group asked his mate: "Who is this old guy?" I told him that Ted had been one of the greatest strikers in the game and his neck muscles were so strong he could head a ball harder than anyone.

Drake offered to demonstrate even though he was in his eighties.

So I threw the ball in the air to Ted and he headed it at the young lad so hard that it knocked him over.

The kids loved it and Ted was asked to repeat the trick but as he did so Peter Osgood came running across shouting: "Tony, what are you doing - you'll kill him!"

I also arranged and played in a few charity football matches, including one for Bobby Moore's Sunday Sport XI against Osgood and a Chelsea Old Stars XI.

In the opening minutes Bill Garner of the Chelsea Old Stars looked like breaking through until Emily Hughes, the former Liverpool star, intervened.

But I then saw a Chelsea boot appear to go over the top of the ball, and Hughes went down with his leg bleeding from stud marks.

It was serious enough for Hughes to be taken to hospital. Such incidents were unheard of in a charity match.

Afterwards I asked Osgood what it was all about. He told me that when they were playing League Football Hughes had got the Chelsea man sent off.

"How long ago was that?" I asked.

Osgood replied: "Oh, about 15 years!"

Such is the tough mentality of many professional footballers - as I found out again when I organised a match for the Ferry Disaster Fund in which Malcolm Macdonald bravely agreed to play to help raise money for the cause despite being almost crippled with arthritis in his knees.

Supermac, famed for scoring goals for Luton Town, Newcastle United, Arsenal and England, could barely run, but the opposition showed little sympathy. They hardly allowed him a kick - it didn't seem to occur to them that the crowd were desperate to see a glimpse of Malcolm's once lethal shooting.

I had the privilege of playing upfront with Macdonald in an All Star XI against a team of former Charlton and Gillingham players. I was only due to appear as a substitute, but George Graham kindly told me to go on in his place for the first-half.

I arranged a couple of other all-star games and played in them both.

One, in which I turned out for a Schoolteachers XI against an All Star XI, was again taken too seriously at times.

An example of this came when I placed a shot past the opposing goalkeeper Geoff Capes, the world's strongest man, but Ray Harford handled the ball on the line to prevent it going into the net.

I was so incensed I ignored the fact that a big crowd was watching and strode up to hammer the penalty into the net, past the huge figure of Geoff Capes.

Geoff Capes is beaten by Tony's surprise burst of speed

The world's strongest man confronts Tony

The Schoolteachers grimly hung on to the lead I had given them, not allowing Steve Coppell, Ossie Ardiles and Co. enough time and space to show off their skills. So I suggested to the referee that he give the All Stars a soft penalty, and once they had scored from the spot, their confidence came flooding back.

Suddenly Coppell and Ardiles were producing flashes of their old magic and they ran out easy winners.

But the Schoolteachers moaned like hell in the dressing room afterwards about the penalty decision!

I actually got to score a 'hat-trick' at Wembley without playing a game there! How is that possible, you may well ask?

Well, I was editor of Football Monthly, Britain's oldest soccer magazine, at the time and had been invited to write a special feature on the Veterans Cup Final at the old Wembley Stadium.

Both teams were willing to name me as one of their substitutes, but were not so keen on the idea of actually bringing me on to play, having never seen me before. This, of course, was quite understandable.

I chose to be a substitute for the team which included former Nottingham Forest star Garry Birtles at centre-forward, and persuaded him to agree to come off two minutes from the end so that I could go on just to have the experience of playing at Wembley. But as the scores were still level in the 88th minute, his manager wouldn't let Garry do the switch.

Ironically, the other team suffered several injuries during the match and I would have got to play had I been a substitute for them!

So how did I score a 'hat-trick'? That came when I converted three penalties out of three in the pre-match kick-about, and I was rather proud of myself because it was against a very good goalkeeper who was taking even the warm-up penalties very seriously.

Back in the Football Monthly office we scratched our heads to think of an appropriate headline for an event that, if I recall, did not produce a single goal in 90 minutes.

I am embarrassed to confess that we highlighted my experience in the story and came up with the heading: 'My Wembley penalty hat-trick.'

CHAPTER TWENTY-SIX

Redknapp's lie shows how tough our job can be

Journalists get a lot of flak, some of which is fully deserved, but they have a very tough job in keeping the public informed, especially when they are lied to by the people they are interviewing.

This was highlighted in the 2012 tax evasion trial of Harry Redknapp, the former Spurs and West Ham manager.

The likable Harry won the hearts of a new generation of television fans last year after showing his love for wife Sandra and telling his amusing stories to be voted King of the Jungle on 'I'm A Celebrity...Get Me Out Of Here'.

But he had said in court six years earlier that he was under no obligation to tell a newspaper reporter the truth.

He claimed that in 2009 he misled News of the World reporter Rob Beasley by saying £93,100 in his account in Monaco was a bonus paid to him by his then Portsmouth chairman Milan Mandaric for the profit made on the sale of Peter Crouch.

Redknapp told the court that he had lied to Beasley to prevent a story appearing in the Sunday tabloid as his Spurs side prepared to face Manchester United in the 2009 League Cup final.

When asked why he referred to payments as bonuses, Redknapp replied: "I wanted to make the point to Mr Beasley that it was paid by my chairman." The Spurs manager said his main concern was to make it clear the payments were not a 'bung' from a football agent but paid legitimately by Mandaric.

He added: "I don't have to tell Mr Beasley the truth. I have to tell police the truth, not Mr Beasley - he's a News of the World reporter."

Redknapp was jointly accused with Mandaric of colluding to conceal payments totalling £189,000 in a Monaco bank account named 'Rosie 47' after Harry's late dog.

The Crown claimed that the payments, made between 2002 and 2004, were taxable since they were employment-related.

Redknapp and Mandaric denied the charges, saying the money was an investment that had nothing to do with Redknapp's employment. Both men were found not guilty after waiting five agonising hours for the jury to give their verdict in a cliff-hanging trial at Southwark Crown Court.

For once an emotionally drained Redknapp* could not come up with a joke for his adoring media and public.

He has treated us to plenty in the past, the best of which have been:

"Even when they had Moore, Hurst and Peters, West Ham's average finish was about 17th position. It just shows how crap the other eight of us were."

"Hartson's got more previous than Jack the Ripper."

"Samassi Abou don't speak the English too good."

"By the look of him, he [Ian Dowie] must have headed a lot of balls."

"Where are we in relation to Europe? Not far from Dover."

"I sorted out the team formation last night lying in bed with the wife. When your husband's as ugly as me, you'd only want to talk football in bed."

There have been so many highs and, in more recent years, lows in the Rednapps' lives since they married in 1967. Sandra's twin sister Patricia died from pneumonia in 2008. Then, in 2016, Harry seriously injured his wife by accidently reversing over her ankle after failing to see her coat was stuck in his car. Two years later the unfortunate Sandra fell ill with the potentially fatal sepsis shortly before Harry won 'I'm A Celebrity'.

Speaking on Piers Morgan's Life Stories on ITV in June this year, Harry revealed: "I nearly pulled out (of going into the jungle). I said look, obviously I'm not going to Australia and do a show if she's not well. It was scary."

Commenting on the breakup between son Jamie and wife Louise in 2017, following Louise's appearance on Strictly Come Dancing, Harry said: "I was choked. Me and Sandra were completely shocked when it happened."

Harry is protective of his wife and wouldn't let her accompany him to court in 2012. He revealed: "Going to jail did cross my mind. The case made Sandra ill - slaughtered her. I wouldn't let her come to court - it would have killed her."

Harry's ordeal reminded me of another court case involving a top football manager, former Manchester United boss Tommy Docherty, who brought a highly-publicised libel case in 1978 over remarks by Scottish international Willie Morgan to the effect that Docherty was, in his opinion, "about the worst manager there has ever been."

Docherty actually had a good record at Manchester United, but he dropped the case on the third day after claims that he had lied in evidence.

At the time I was Sports Editor of the Lancashire Evening Telegraph in Blackburn and attended a local dinner at which Docherty had been booked to speak immediately after the trial. There was deadly silence as he got up to talk, but he won the audience over and immediately had them in fits of laughter by saying: "You're not going to believe a word of this."

When Tommy and I chatted years later he came out with an updated quip about his court appearance by telling me: "I admitted to the judge I'd lied on oath, but he didn't believe me, either." And he added: "The guy operating the lift at the Old Bailey asked me if I was going down and I said 'I hope not'." No wonder I love talking to The Doc!

One of my favourite Docherty quotes came after he was sacked by Aston Villa chairman Doug Ellis. Tommy later recalled how his chairman had initially said he was right behind his manager. His response was: "I told him I'd sooner have him in front of me where I could see him."

And following his unsuccessful spell as manager of Rotherham United, Docherty declared: "I promised the chairman I'd get them out of the Second Division (now the Championship) and I did. I took them into the Third."

Other great Docherty jokes were:

"Elton John decided he wanted to rename Watford and call it Queen of the South."

"They offered me a handshake of £10,000 to settle amicably. I told them that they would have to be a lot more amicable than that."

Referring to Ray Wilkins: "He can't run, he can't tackle and he can't head the ball. The only time he goes forward is for the toss."

And on Paul Gascoigne: "He's a disgrace...30 going on six!"

Having such a great sense of humour, and being prepared to poke fun at himself got The Doc out of some awkward situations during his long career as it did Redknapp, who I also found to be very entertaining at his post-match Press conferences - win, lose or draw!

Docherty is best remembered for his time at Manchester United, where he saved them from relegation and, after going down the next season in 1973-4, promptly won the Second Division. There followed successive FA Cup final appearances, the latter a great 2-1 win over Liverpool to deny them the treble in 1976, but he was sacked a year later in July 1977.

This was due mainly to pressure from players' wives after Docherty had an affair with the wife of club physio Laurie Brown. The fact that this was not some wild fling, and that Tommy had left his wife of 27 years to live with Mary Brown was not enough to save him.

He and the affable Mary, 18 years his junior, showed their devotion to each other by marrying, and have enjoyed a very happy life together ever since.

The Doc has remained razor sharp in his nineties and talks a lot of sense. He predicted Jose Mourinho wouldn't last long at Manchester United, saying: "You can't argue with his record but I think he goes over the top with his criticism of players."

Docherty reckoned that Mourinho should have off-loaded £89m midfielder Paul Pogba with whom he had a feud. He said: "Mourinho needed to show he was in charge by getting rid of Pogba

"Pogba kept blowing hot and cold. United should never have re-signed him. Sir Alex Ferguson let him go for a reason. The club have signed too many prima donnas and it remains to be seen if manager Ole Gunnar Solskjaer will be strong enough to handle multi-million pound players. He must be given the backing of the Board, and allowed time to prove himself.

"It doesn't make sense to me to have executive vice chairman Ed Wooward, who has not played professional football, influencing who United sign. He has already made some costly mistakes and I believe he is skating on thin ice."

So how does Docherty feel about the club being owned and financially exploited by the Glazer family whose take-over was structured by former banker Woodward and resulted in £487m of borrowing.

He told me: "In my view it was a big mistake to sell United to the Glazers. Under them, the club took out massive loans and that has been a huge hurdle to overcome. They have fallen a long way behind Manchester City, who I now prefer to watch."

The one-time Scotland manager still takes a keen interest in international football. Asked if England had appointed the right manager in Gareth Southgate, he replied: "I think so. He played at the highest level and can prove to be a successful manager, too. But England are not yet good enough to win the World Cup, though they might be in contention if their young players mature. That could take anything up to ten years."

Tommy feels the FA have made several errors with previous England managers and believes Fabio Capello was stabbed in the back when he departed in February, 2012 - on the same day Redknapp was found not guilty in his court case.

Docherty told me: "By not telling Capello of their intention to take the captaincy away from John Terry until after making their decision, the FA put their manager in an almost impossible situation.

"I find it hard to believe that they did not know Capello would feel forced to quit. Capello was right to support Terry on the basis that a man is innocent until proved guilty. I wonder if the FA had a hidden agenda in not backing a manager who was costing them £6million a year."

Docherty added: "Normally the FA would have been severely criticised for making yet another insensitive blunder and acting like a bunch of amateurs, but because many journalists and fans did not feel Capello was the right man for the job, the FA got away with it."

During my career as a journalist, Docherty - and Redknapp - were always very friendly and co-operative with me. I remember when I took over as Head of Sport at Sunday Sport that our newly-appointed big name writer Peter Batt left just before our launch and I had to write the stories for the first issue myself.

We needed an explosive article that was going to be a 'must read' for most sports fans, and The Doc came up trumps by giving me an outspoken exclusive on which managers were in line for the sack.

Former England manager Bobby Robson was also very helpful when I was Sports Editor of the Fleet Street News

Agency. I found two of his successors, Terry Venables and Glenn Hoddle, to be less free with their time.

Robson kindly granted me one-to-one exclusive interviews after his Press conferences because he knew that, as I worked for a freelance agency, I could not market the same quotes he had given to the rest of the media.

My one regret is that when I took my impressionable young son James along with me to one of Robson's Press conferences I did not introduce James to him properly because I was so anxious to get some quotes first.

In fact, Bobby told me he didn't have much time that day so I had to be quick which meant James never did get introduced to him.

* Harry Redknapp brought out a new book entitled 'The World According to Harry' on May 30, 2019. There are several other interesting books featuring both Redknapp and Tommy Docherty available on Amazon.co.uk

CHAPTER TWENTY-SEVEN

Violated by News of the World

I was very sad to see the demise of the News of the World, especially as I worked there for more than a year as a part-time sports sub-editor, being one of several 'Saturday casuals' brought in to help cope with the busiest day of a Sunday paper's week.

But I have no sympathy for those found guilty of phone hacking. In my day reporters would find out facts by asking probing questions, even if it meant standing around for hours to catch a few minutes (sometimes only seconds) with the people they needed to speak to.

The News of the World's publishers News International had to admit their guilt and pay out huge sums to many people whose phones were hacked into, including £300,000 in damages, plus the same amount in legal costs, to singer Charlotte Church and her parents.

The scandal left a lot of the hacking victims feeling violated as was pointed out by Abi Titmuss, who I have referred to meeting earlier in this book.

Abi admitted that her career as a pin-up model before becoming a serious actress was mainly due to the media.

But she stressed that the Press had no right to be so intrusive to the point where her life was no longer her own.

She said: "The Press created me, but they almost destroyed me emotionally and my family.

"I know for a long time they were hacking my phone, but nobody believed me. I changed my number lots of times, but that didn't stop it.

"I've had journalists who I've met since say 'We used to make up things all the time'. My self-esteem had become so low and I had become so unhappy because of what was happening.

"I sued News International for hacking my phone - they thought they were untouchable."

Discussing the situation with Andrew Neil on BBC's 'This Week' in February, 2012, she explained: "The reason there was a public outcry was that if it was just celebrities who had their phones hacked people would have shrugged and it would not have been such a huge deal.

"But ordinary people were involved - grieving parents who never sought fame."

Abi was referring to the disgraceful case in which the parents of a murdered British teenager were given false hope that she was still alive.

The Leveson investigation was ordered after revelations that a private detective working for the News of the World hacked the phone of 13-year-old Milly Dowler while she was missing.

Milly's mother Sally Dowler described the moment she got through to her daughter's previously full voicemail.

"It clicked through onto her voicemail, so I heard her voice... And it was just like, 'she has picked up her voicemails - she is alive'."

That was the final nail in the coffin of the News of the World, although it was, of course, replaced on Sundays by its former sister paper The Sun. After 168 years in print, the News of the World brought out its final edition on July 10th, 2011, but seven months later News International's Rupert Murdoch published the first Sunday edition of the Sun in February, 2012.

It promised 'trust' and 'decency', yet, as Abi said: "The trouble with tabloid culture is that it requires a constant supply of victims like errant MPs, misbehaving footballers and fallen rock stars - when ordinary people become involved then things are different."

Ironically, the Press, led by The Sun on Sunday, have recently been campaigning for social media sites such as Facebook to be more responsible.

Referring to the need to ban self-harm and suicide sites, The Sun on Sunday raged, in an editorial on February 10th, 2019: "Arrogant social media bosses have made billions from a lawless culture which has left many children in despair."

CHAPTER TWENTY-EIGHT

Why we 'rubbished' our own stories

My life at Sunday Sport in the late 1980s was bizarre, as you might imagine.

When I saw the advertisement seeking the 'Head of Sport' for a new national tabloid newspaper, I thought it would be a serious publication. Only after I landed the job did I fully realise that Sunday Sport was going to be a downmarket version of the Sun, with news pages crammed full of pictures of topless models and sexy stories.

I vowed to keep the sport serious so I was delighted when we took on Bobby Moore, and gave him the title of Sports Editor, with me being Assistant Editor in charge of sport. It meant I was the boss of England's 1966 World Cup-winning captain!

I promptly recruited other sports stars as columnists, including tennis ace Jo Durie and athlete Fatima Whitbread. I also brought in a host of former footballers such as John Charles, Peter Osgood, Alan Hudson, Tommy Smith and Frank McLintock to write Saturday match reports, all on a very small budget!

Before settling on Jo Durie I had approached Virginia Wade at the Wimbledon Championships. But she appeared to be rather disdainful about the whole idea, and it seemed obvious the fee on offer would be so derisory to her that she'd almost certainly scoff at it.

Only after she said she wasn't interested and I was walking away did she call back to me: "Anyway, how much are you offering?"

I saved face by replying "You'll never know now, Virginia."

I also had the task of escorting models Samatha Fox and Linda Lusardi and DJ Tony Blackburn into a party Sunday Sport threw at Stringfellows night club. It was a tough job!

As I mentioned briefly in a previous chapter, there was a massive queue outside Stringfellows and I had to walk along it to rescue any VIPs who were supposed to gain immediate entrance.

One of the VIPs I found in the queue was Tony Blackburn, but by now the nightclub was packed. I told him: "Come with me, Tony, but if you think this is a big crowd outside just you wait until you get in. It's heaving with people." A lot of them were scantily clad girls.

When Sunday Sport was launched in 1986 the staff would be instructed by our own management to phone up various radio shows and 'rubbish' ourselves by telling them how dreadful the paper's stories were. This was reverse psychology, aimed at arousing listeners' interest so much that they felt compelled to buy the paper!

Sunday Sport would run ridiculous stories such as 'Woman pregnant 60 years gives birth to old age pensioner'.

The paper printed what it claimed was a picture of a B-17 World War Two bomber plane on the moon. The photograph, supposedly taken from thousands of miles away, wasn't even blurred.

Sure enough, Sunday Sport readers wrote in to complain, but not about it being a fake picture! They pointed out it was NOT a B-17, but a B-29.

And while other papers were asking whether the Queen should abdicate, Sunday Sport readers already knew it was a pointless debate because we had told them that her body had allegedly been taken over by aliens years earlier.

Some of our readers even accepted our ludicrous claims that a double-decker London bus had been found frozen in the Antarctic ice and that Hitler was a woman.

Although I came to loathe the way all this distracted from our serious sports reporting, I was, nevertheless, proud that I was part of a dedicated editorial team which helped to launch a new national paper and build up a circulation of almost half a million from scratch.

We printed Sunday Sport from the offices of the Northampton Evening Chronicle each Saturday, and when we did our dummy run I was in charge of the whole sports operation.

This meant working with a completely new staff and having to get the paper on the printing presses an hour after the Saturday afternoon football programme had finished, including working out the league tables.

Editor-in-chief Mike Gabbert had suggested that we get famous former soccer players to report on matches so it was necessary for our sub-editors to speak to these personalities at half-time and again at the end of the game.

As a safety measure, I ensured that the personalities were sitting in the Press box next to qualified soccer writers, who telephoned over factual reports before handing the phone to the former players to give their opinions.

My team of sub-editors, a collection of freelance 'casuals', found it to be a frantic operation.

The staff of the Northampton Chronicle were sitting at the far end of their editorial offices having a laugh at our expense. But they weren't laughing when we brought out the first ever edition on time with everything in place.

Sunday Sport's publishers were David Sullivan and brothers David and Ralph Gold, with advertising the responsibility of Sullivan's then protégée Karren Brady. The four of them went on to take control at Birmingham City Football Club and later West Ham United.

Sunday Sport was still going strong when I departed, together with the rest of the full-time sports staff, in protest at the farcical stories appearing on the paper's news pages.

But a few years later the Sport and its new sister publication Daily Sport began to lose their appeal and circulation dwindled. Sunday Sport's publication was suspended from April 1, 2011 after Sport Media Group ceased trading and appointed administrators, with all 90 staff being made redundant.

Former owner David Sullivan stepped in to buy Sunday Sport, but not the Daily Sport. Publication resumed on May 8, 2011 under a new company, Sunday Sport (2011) Ltd, and the paper took on its own website. But a full time staff of just eight occupied their new Manchester office which was a similar number to when we started back in 1986.

Despite all the young topless girls associated with Sunday Sport, I had been happy to spend my free time with a respectable divorced mother of three boys called Linda.

You may recall I mentioned how she did not recognise Frank Bruno when I took her to the Sports Personality of the Year awards at Wembley.

At the same event Linda was photographed with Nick Faldo, who she did recognise, and John Sillett, the manager of Coventry City, the shock team of the year after beating Spurs to win the 1987 FA Cup in their first ever final after 104 years of trying.

Sillett was standing next to Linda, grinning, as a picture was about to be taken when suddenly his smile changed to a rather pained expression after she had spoken to him.

"What on earth did you say to him?" I asked her as we walked away. "Nothing," she replied. "I just said 'I've got no idea who on earth you are'."

Sillett obviously had an ego and felt that people should know who he was. Several years later, a now portly, balding Sillett recalled in the build up to the 2012 FA Cup third round: "I'm reminded of our cup win every time I walk down the street in Coventry, Liverpool and all sorts of places. I'm recognised all the time. People say 'Hey, Cup Final 1987'. They even remember the date."

The likeable former Sky Blues boss revealed that by beating Manchester United on route to Wembley they almost brought about the demise of United manager Alex Ferguson.

Sillett disclosed: "Alex said 'It's the nearest I've ever been to getting the sack'."

John claimed that Coventry's second equaliser in a 3-2 extra-time victory was "the best goal to be scored at Wembley - a diving header by Keith Houchen from a magnificent cross by Dave Bennett."

Perhaps a slight exaggeration, John!

CHAPTER TWENTY-NINE

'I was drained and depressed' says Flintoff

Sports stars today are treated like kings compared to those of bygone years. But, with the mega bucks, comes more media attention, stress and sometimes depression.

Among those who have suffered from the intense pressures have been cricket ace Freddie Flintoff and footballer-turned-actor Vinnie Jones.

I have met them both and saw some evidence of the strain that fan adoration and the media spotlight can place on them.

I was with Flintoff only briefly when my newspaper was invited to interview him at a book signing so I went along with my colleague Ross Basham, who was covering the event.

We were staggered to see such a massive crowd turn up to buy Flintoff's book and have it signed by the England hero himself. It took him ages to sign all the books, pose for pictures and answer questions.

Freddie was charming, but I thought I detected behind the smiles a trace of anxiety from the Ashes hero, who has since revealed that the pressure of Test cricket left him fighting depression and led to booze binges.

Flintoff has admitted to being at his lowest ebb in 2007 when he was sacked as England's vice-captain following a drunken pedalo ride during the World Cup.

He confessed: "Sportsmen experience unbelievable highs and dramatic lows. You never think that the lows could turn into depression but for some it all gets too much."

Tony and colleague Ross Basham join Freddie Flintoff at his book signing

Talking about that Caribbean nightmare in a BBC1 documentary, 'The Hidden Side of Sport', screened on January 11, 2012, he said: "I didn't know what I was doing, and all I was thinking about on the field and throughout that World Cup was that I wanted to retire.

"When I took wickets I used to like a celebration. But on that trip I just stood there. I couldn't muster the energy to do anything."

It was all a far cry from when he became a national hero by inspiring England's Ashes triumph in 2005. But his fortunes changed dramatically as he captained England to a humiliating 5-0 defeat in the Ashes series of 2006-7 in Australia.

Flintoff revealed that on Christmas Eve 2006 he cried his eyes out and told his dad he couldn't take it any more - that he couldn't keep playing. He added: "I dusted myself down and carried on, but I was never the same player again."

Freddie confessed that he turned to drink long before he quit playing in 2010 through injury. He admitted: "I was so low at the time (of the pedalo incident) it might have pushed me over the edge."

Vinnie Jones had previously told how he'd been hit by suicidal depression after biting a journalist in 1998.

He said: "I'd let everybody down. I took a gun to the woods with the intention of firing it. I was tired of causing people stress - it was a cheap way out, but I did think everyone would be better off if I was out of the way and stopped causing them trouble."

His dog saved him from pulling the trigger. Speaking to Piers Morgan on Life Stories on ITV in November, 2009, he said he changed his mind when his Jack Russell Tessie trotted up to him and gave him a pleading look.

Hard man Jones, a member of the Wimbledon Crazy Gang who helped the Dons win the 1998 FA Cup final against all the odds, was sent off 12 times in his career.

I interviewed Vinnie after one of his on-field misdemeanours caused him to see red once again, and I feared that my questions about the incident would cause him to erupt with fury. Fortunately, Jones had calmed down by the time we spoke and I saw the other, humorous side of him. We finished up having a good laugh!

CHAPTER THIRTY

Jimmy White and the waistcoat

I spent four very happy years as Controller of Information at BSkyB and often joked about having 200 people working under me because I was on the third floor and they were on the two floors below!

My main job was performing an important public relations exercise to increase awareness of the Eurosport channel. I did this by arranging a variety of events and issuing a stream of press releases, many of them containing interviews I carried out with sports stars who appeared on Eurosport programmes.

I was responsible for publicising one of Sky and Eurosport's biggest sports events, the first World Snooker Masters, which was the richest snooker tournament to be held, with £1million prize money, and the first to feature women players as well as men at that level.

The initial Press Conference in November, 1990 saw me interview on camera world champions Stephen Hendry and Alison Fisher, Jimmy White, promoter Barry Hearn and presenter Dickie Davies.

In order to add a touch of glamour, it was decided to let the contestants wear brightly coloured, trendy waistcoats.

So I contacted a Savile Row tailor and arranged to hire about 25 waistcoats from him.

Jimmy White, then among the top players in the world, look a shine to one of them and was reluctant to part with this colourful item of clothing at the end of the tournament until I told him he would have to pay for it – and how much it would cost him!

Football manager Ron Atkinson was another who gave me a problem. He had agreed to pose in a Sky cap for a publicity picture at the next match his Sheffield Wednesday team played in London, but when the photographer and I approached him before kick-off at Charlton, he said there wasn't enough time and he would do it in Sheffield instead!

Atkinson wasn't made aware that, when news of this got back to the Sky office, concern was expressed about whether perhaps we might want someone more flexible to be part of our team!

One of my ideas at Sky was to promote our 1990 World Cup coverage by creating our own man-sized version of the competition mascot Ciao.

So I hired a tailor to make us a costume, complete with a football-shaped head, and then all I needed was someone to wear it. There were no volunteers which meant I had to don it myself to appear on TV as a giant mascot.

The person who actually found the tailor to carry out this task was my mother! I needed a temporary assistant who I knew I could rely on so took on my mum as a 'casual' shortly after she had retired from her job as a secretary.

I didn't tell anybody in the Sky office that my new assistant was my mother, but they may have guessed when she kept straightening my tie and on one occasion told me to adjust my trousers!

My job sometimes enabled me to help promote worthy causes, and I organised a charity football match in which the likes of Ossie Ardiles and Steve Coppell played. Afterwards I interviewed both Ossie and Steve on camera.

Interviewing the great Ossie Ardiles

Surprisingly, I did not have much contact with the long-serving anchor-men of Sky's football coverage, Richard Keys and Andy Gray, who were hauled off air in January 2011 following sexist comments about female football officials and executives.

Keys resigned after Gray lost his job.

The pair were originally disciplined for making sexist remarks about the female assistant referee Sian Massey before a match between Wolves and Liverpool. They were off air but recorded on tape and it was leaked to the media.

Gray was dismissed after new footage came to light that showed him making suggestive remarks to a female co-host. The pressure to also take action against Keys increased when another clip appeared to show him talking in sexiest terms about a former girlfriend of the pundit Jamie Redknapp. Keys resigned soon afterwards.

It's amazing how swiftly the axe can fall on even those playing massive roles in a multi-million pound industry.

As most of my time was devoted to public relations at Eurosport, I appeared on Sky sports channels only a few times, and ironically most of my television appearances came on BBC News 24 some years later.

The Beeb engaged me as an early morning analyst, commenting on the sports news of the week and handing out criticism where necessary as I did to Manchester United boss Alex Ferguson over his famous boot kicking rage which injured his own player David Beckham.

One of my TV appearances on an evening programme nearly didn't happen because of the fussiness of the producer. I was due to talk about the England football team and at the 11th hour this producer got the bright idea that I should be standing in front of the twin towers of Wembley Stadium.

So he sent a car and off we sped from South East London, in rush hour traffic, with only an hour to get there for my scheduled slot.

After a mad rush, we just made it with a few minutes of the programme remaining. I still can't understand why the producer risked missing out on the whole thing for the sake of having Wembley in the background!

I also used to be on screen regularly as a guest on Mirror Group Newspapers' fledgling LIVE TV British cable television channel, set up in 1995.

The channel's boss was Kelvin MacKenzie, who after editing the Sun moved to BSkyB but left them within a few months.

The station had previously been headed by Janet Street-Porter, who wanted to establish L!VE TV as an alternative, youth-orientated channel. She clashed with MacKenzie over programme content and soon departed, leaving him in sole charge.

MacKenzie went down-market by introducing nightly editions of 'Topless Darts', featuring bare-chested women playing darts on a beach, 'The Weather in Norwegian' (with a young, blonde, bikini-clad Scandinavian woman presenting weather forecasts in both English and Norwegian), and stock exchange reports from Tiffany, a young female presenter who would strip as she read out the latest share prices.

I appeared on the channel's more conservative programmes, commenting on various sports topics before ending up playing some daft game in a one-to-one challenge against the celebrity guest I was appearing with. This hardly brought me countrywide fame because the station had a budget of only £2,000 an hour and was never watched by more than an average of 200,000 viewers.

CHAPTER THIRTY-ONE

'Why I married Jacklin despite his fling'

Sport can play hell with married life - and golfers on tour are some of the biggest 'victims'.

I spent a long conversation sympathising with Scottish star Sandy Lyle about his marriage ending in divorce, and, after speaking to former Open Champion Tony Jacklin and his second wife, I could even understand him having an affair with a teenage girl soon after the death of his first wife.

But I had less sympathy for fellow Brit Nick Faldo over his marriage break-ups and none at all for American icon Tiger Woods, whose wife suddenly discovered that the world's most successful golfer loved playing around so much he sometimes had as many birdies off the course as on it!

I was given an exclusive interview by Jacklin and his second wife Astrid, which made a double-page spread, containing my by-line, in the Daily Star in September 1989.

Astrid, who married Britain's most successful Ryder Cup captain only eight months after his first wife Vivien died of a brain haemorrhage while driving her car in Spain, told me how they coped when death struck again by depriving them of a baby son.

Norwegian-born Astrid, formerly married to Bee Gees guitarist Alan Kendall, also spoke about what it was like to live with the ghost of Tony's first marriage.

She said: "Vivien is always going to be part of our lives. I realise that when you have loved someone for so long, you don't forget them just because they are no longer alive.

"If you've spent more than 20 years with them and had three kids with them, they're still part of you and the memories will always be there."

Astrid had to come through other traumas soon after Tony breezed into her life. She recalled: "Within two weeks of me meeting Tony in Spain, the story of his fling with a teenage waitress broke.

"He'd already told me about it, and I accepted it as something that happened when he was still beside himself with grief over his wife's death."

Despite the 'sex romp' headlines following 16-year-old waitress Donna Nethven's kiss-and-tell revelations about the three-month affair which started six weeks after Vivien's death, Astrid insisted: "I had complete belief in Tony."

Jacklin said: "I have been tremendously fortunate to find someone so understanding. If Astrid hadn't been so right I wouldn't have asked her not to go back to America after knowing her only three days."

He and Astrid also had to overcome the tragedy of losing their baby in July, 1989.

When Astrid began having contractions four months early during the British Open in Troon they needed to get to London quickly to see her doctor, so Jack Nicklaus lent them his private jet. But nothing could be done and Astrid miscarried.

Tony tried to be philosophical. He said: "I suppose life is kind of like golf. It's a little like Trevino's chip-in. Anything can happen to you, any time, so what's the point of trying to understand it? You can't make sense of it anyway, so why try?"

When I met Faldo, the winner of six majors, we did not touch on the subject of his marriage break-ups, but I spoke in depth to Lyle about his divorce.

Sandy, who triumphed in the British Open in 1985 and the Masters in 1988, was deeply upset by his split from his wife Christine, also a professional golfer, in 1987.

He told me: "Golf has made me a lot of money, yet it has cost me a divorce and so much upset. But I'm lucky to have my kids."

I tried to console him with words of sympathy and encouragement about how better things lay in store for him. I also threw in a joke: "Man is not complete until he's married and then he's finished. But practice makes perfect."

Faldo tried to laugh off his marriage problems with a few jokes of his own.

His best were: "We were happily married for eight months - unfortunately we were married for four and a half years!" and "I never advise anyone to go to war or to get married."

Faldo met his first wife, Melanie Rockall, when he was 21. They wed in 1979, but five years later they split up after she discovered he was having a relationship with his manager's secretary, Gill Bennett.

He then married Gill in 1986, and the couple had three children, Natalie, Matthew and Georgia. They parted in 1995 after Faldo began a relationship with 20-year-old American golfing student Brenna Cepelak.

The three-year affair with Cepelak ended when Faldo met Valerie Bercher. The spurned Cepelak showed her anger by pounding Faldo's Porsche 959 with a golf club, causing £10,000 damage.

Faldo's relationship with Valerie, a Swiss PR agent, began in 1998 when they met at the European Masters golf tournament. She left her fiancé Olivier Delaloye, married Faldo in July 2001 at his Windsor home, and two years later they had a daughter, Emma Scarlet.

But it was announced in May 2006 that Faldo had filed for divorce and again the Press were having a field day at his expense.

Little wonder that journalists are not his favourite people. But when I helped to entertain him at a Sports Writers Association dinner, where I was a member of the organising committee, he was at his most affable and charming.

I feel that Faldo got off lightly compared to Tiger Woods over the repercussions of his relationships with women, especially regarding the damage to his pocket.

Woods paid a very heavy price for cheating several times on wife Elin Nordegren, who divorced him in August 2010.

The Swedish former model is believed to have been paid £100million as part of the settlement and Tiger's reputation was severely tarnished. But he had nobody to blame but himself!

CHAPTER THIRTY-TWO

Curtain went up as singer was being spanked

Some of the biggest names in show business have suffered from stage fright, including Barbra Streisand, Rod Stewart, Colin Firth, Geoffrey Rush, Frankie Howerd and even Sir Laurence Olivier.

Stephen Fry revealed that it forced him to contemplate suicide, while singer Carly Simon tried to overcome the problem by having her bottom spanked!

TV presenter, award winning actor and singer Matthew Kelly has also been plagued by stage fright, as he told me when we chatted at Richmond Theatre.

He said: "It is something which many actors and singers suffer from. I still get scared about performing as an actor, and years ago I lost my nerve for singing on stage."

Kelly, best known as the host of ITV's 'Stars In Their Eyes', expanded on the subject when appearing on the 'Alan Titchmarsh Show' on ITV in March, 2012. He explained: "If you are nervous and get actual stage fright your singing voice is the first thing to go.

"It's awful. Even now I'm terrified of going on stage when I'm doing a play. Every morning I wake up and think

'Please God, don't make me do that.' But the minute you set foot on stage it's the greatest ride of your life.

A confident looking Matthew Kelly (left) has suffered from stage fright

"Actors are the most wonderful people to be with. They're funny, they're kind, they're supportive, they're generous - and they're bonkers!"

But Barbra Streisand, whose stage fright caused her to stay away from the concert stage for more than 25 years, didn't appear to show much support to the late Dudley Moore when, in 1995, she fired him from the film she was directing, 'The Mirror Has Two Faces', for having trouble remembering his lines.

It was devastating for Dudley, who two years later had open-heart surgery. He suffered four strokes, and doctors discovered a build-up of calcium on his brain, an irreversible condition worsened by drugs and alcohol. He died in 2002, aged 66.

Miss Streisand, who probably did not know about his health problems when she worked with Moore, has always been a notorious perfectionist. She had said years earlier while emerging as a new teenage sensation: "I wasn't trying to be difficult - it just came naturally."

My view is that Miss Streisand might have been more understanding with Dudley Moore, especially as she had also failed to remember her lines on one memorable occasion.

She had forgotten the lyrics to one of her songs during a 1967 Central Park concert, which resulted in her no longer performing live for almost three decades.

She said: "Some performers forget the words all the time, but they somehow have humour about it. I didn't have a sense of humour about it. I was quite shocked."

Even Sir Laurence Olivier, the greatest actor of his time, worried frantically that he would fail to remember his lines as he reached late middle age. It got so bad that the stage manager had to push him on stage every night in one run at London's National Theatre.

Stephen Fry actually walked out on the West End play 'Cell Mates' in 1995 and contemplated suicide.

The comedian and writer revealed: "I went into my garage, sealed the door with a duvet and got into my car. I sat there for at least two hours, with my hands on the ignition key. It was a suicide attempt - not a cry for help."

But instead of gassing himself, Fry fled to Belgium. He recalled: "I really believed I would never come back to

England. But after a week I secretly returned and went to hospital where a doctor told me that I'm bipolar."

Fry, speaking in a BBC2 documentary about being a depressive, added: "For the first time, at the age of 37, I had a diagnosis that explained the massive highs and miserable lows I've lived with all my life."

His walk-out after only three days in the role of KGB agent George Blake meant that Simon Gray's play, which also starred Rik Mayall, was killed off.

Speaking of his decision to go AWOL, Fry said: "That was play fright, not stage fright - it's a very different thing."

One actor, Ian Holm, actually gave up during a performance! He walked off stage and refused to return in 'The Iceman Cometh' in 1976. He explained in a 1998 interview: "Something just snapped. Once the concentration goes, the brain literally closes down."

Colin Firth and Geoffrey Rush have also admitted to suffering stage fright, which is doubly ironic after the acclaim they both received in 'The King's Speech', the Oscar-winning film about the chronic stammer of George VI (Firth) and his treatment with an Australian speech therapist (Rush).

Firth recalled how on opening night of his stage appearance at the Donmar Warehouse in 1999 he became so scared that he locked himself in the toilet. Then he went out of the theatre to get some air, and accidentally shut the fire door behind him, five minutes before he was due on stage.

He recalled: "I was forced to go round the front of the theatre, through the audience - the very people I was terrified of facing." In his panic he couldn't remember the pass code to get backstage and had to plead to be allowed in.

Rush admitted having similar problems in the early 1990s. He recalled: "I suffered dread-inducing panic attacks before going on stage - then I got an international film career and they sort of disappeared."

Rod Stewart was so nervous when performing at New York's Fillmore East Theatre back in 1968 that he sang the whole of the first song from behind a pile of speakers.

The most bizarre method I've heard about for overcoming stage fright is that used by singer Carly Simon. She resorted to poking herself in the hand with safety pins, and having her bottom spanked before performing live.

But her secret ritual was accidentally revealed in the most embarrassing manner when she appeared at a concert in 1996 to mark then-US President Bill Clinton's 50th birthday.

Simon, already a popular recording artist, with a number of hit songs including 'Anticipation', 'You're So Vain' and 'Nobody Does It Better', confessed: "The orchestra's horn section all took turns spanking me. But during the spank the curtain went up."

The tall, attractive singer-songwriter, with the most sexy of pouts, whose admirers were said to include Jeremy Irons, Mick Jagger, Jack Nicholson, Kris Kristofferson and

Cat Stevens, must have looked quite a sight. I wonder what Bill Clinton said to her afterwards!

CHAPTER THIRTY-THREE

Claire was chatted up by US President

Few women would deliberately put on two stones in six weeks, but talented actress and singer Claire Sweeney did!

The then 37-year-old Liverpudlian beauty piled on the pounds in 2009 for a TV documentary called 'My Big Fat Diet' as she soared from 9st 12lb to 11st 10lb.

She told me that she would eat pizzas, chicken, chips and eggs Benedict. And Claire became so big that some people thought she was pregnant.

But being larger had its advantages because men found her more ample breasts a big attraction, and those guys who had previously thought the gorgeous star was out of their league suddenly felt confident enough to approach her.

The charming Claire said: "My bra size went from a 'C' cup to a 'G' cup. My boobs were magnificent and I'd never been chatted up by so many men."

One of those who tried a chat-up line on her when she was in her trimmer shape was Bill Clinton while he was U.S. President, but Claire wasn't impressed.

She was wearing a cheeky Dangerous Liaisons-style costume at a fancy dress party in Russia, hosted by Cliff

Richard, when Clinton approached her, dressed as an admiral.

Sweeney, who was at the party with her boyfriend Tony Hibbard, told Channel Five's 'The Wright Stuff': "Clinton came over and started chatting me up. I thought: 'You dirty dog'."

Despite being told by his bodyguard that it was time to go, the then 62-year-old President refused to do so and returned to talk to her.

The conversation went as follows:

Claire: 'You don't want to go, do you?'

Clinton: 'How can you tell?'

Claire: 'Because your left leg is dancing'."

Clinton allegedly told her: 'My middle leg will be dancing soon!'

Sweeney joked: "I shook his hand, but decided I was going home with a clean dress that night!"

White House intern Monica Lewinsky had claimed that her blue dress had been soiled by The President during their affair in 1997.

CHAPTER THIRTY-FOUR

Rowling and Lloyd Webber were sued

My adventure fantasy book 'The Secret Potion' was hailed by author Jessica Duchen and late actress June Whitfield as an ideal follow up to Harry Potter - but I did not lift any of author J.K. Rowling's story lines or ideas.

Ironically, it was Rowling, probably the most successful and wealthiest author in the world, who had to defend herself against charges of plagiarism.

A law suit was brought in 2002 by American author Nancy Stouffer, who claimed that there was a striking resemblance between her character 'Larry Potter' and Rowling's 'Harry Potter'. Although it was accepted that there were similarities between the spectacle-wearing Larry Potter and Harry Potter, Stouffer, whose books published in the 1980s, lost her case and an appeal three years later.

Then, in 2011, the estate of Adrian Jacobs, a writer who died in 1997, brought a plagiarism case against Rowling, but it was dismissed by a U.S. judge after the estate's lawyers failed to meet a deadline for paying the first portion of £1.5million into court as security for costs.

The claim was that Rowling repeated parts of Jacobs's 'Willie the Wizard' in 'Harry Potter and the Goblet of Fire'. The lawyers acting on behalf of his estate referred to the fact that Jacob's book involved a school for wizards and wizards travelling on trains. Rowling said she had never heard of Willie the Wizard before the copyright claim was taken out.

Judge Shira Sheindlin wrote in her ruling: "The contrast between the total concept and feel of the works is so stark that any serious comparison of the two strains credulity."

There have also been many copyright infringement cases brought by musicians and composers. Andrew Lloyd Webber was sued in 1998 by Baltimore songwriter Ray Repp, who claimed that the theme song from 'The Phantom of The Opera' was taken from his song 'Till You'. But a jury cleared Webber of plagiarism. There were also claims that Phantom closely resembled some of the musical phrases in Puccini's opera 'The Girl of the Golden West' and the Puccini estate sued Webber. The suit was settled out of court, with the details not being made public.

It is hard to prove plagiarism because it can be claimed that most pieces of work bare some resemblance to something else on the basis that most things have already been thought of before. But there is, of course, a huge difference between a writer being influenced by another author or composer and lifting someone else's work almost completely.

Actor and TV presenter Matthew Kelly, who I once chatted to at a theatre function in Surrey, gave an insight into how he is influenced by other performers.

Speaking on 'The Alan Titchmarsh Show' on ITV, he said: "People always say never watch other actors do the part you are going to play. But I always watch them. I nick all the good bits

"When I was doing 'Who's Afraid of Virginia Woof' people said 'don't watch Richard Burton do it'. Now, am I ever going to do it like Richard Burton? I'd be more like Elizabeth Taylor.

"It helps you to learn to watch others. There was a great line in a play about Eric Morecambe - 'There's nothing original until you make it your own'. I think that's absolutely true so that's how I justify my 'plagiarism'."

CHAPTER THIRTY-FIVE

Show business is brutal says Philippa - and some advice for Simon Cowell

Critically acclaimed West End actress and singer Philippa Healey revealed to me how brutal show business can be.

The talented Lancashire lass's soprano voice was described by Sir Cameron Mackintosh as "absolutely magnificent" after he cast her as the grown up Cosette in the record-breaking London production of 'Les Miserables' at the Palace Theatre.

But she told me: "Show business is brutal. It's an over-crowded industry in which casting directors are often very picky. I will advise my children to go into different professions."

Philippa has experienced many highs and lows. She reflected: "I never got that really lucky big break. I was auditioned for the leading female role of Christine in Phantom of the Opera three times and on each occasion reached the last two, only to miss out. I also just missed landing a recording contact with Decca that could have resulted in stardom.

"It's so frustrating. One producer told me I was too confident!"

Philippa, who combines piano playing and comedic charm with superb vocals in her variety performances, has been a soloist with the National Symphony Orchestra.

There have been many other memorable moments - one of which was meeting fellow opera singer Nick Allen when working on a show together. They fell in love and are now happily married, with two children, Nathaniel, aged six, and Rose, two.

Actor Brian Capron can sympathise with Philippa.

He and Barrie Foster were dumped off 'Jack The Ripper' in the 1988 Anglo-American television co-production.

Filming was halted in December 1987 after American network CBS became involved, resulting in most of the original cast and crew being paid off.

CBS wanted the new mini-series to feature actors well known to American viewers so Foster and Capron were replaced by Michael Caine and Lewis Collins as Chief Inspector Frederick Abberline and his partner George Godley.

Brian told me: "I was really choked as it would have been my international break."

Several DVD editions of Jack the Ripper include, as extra features, twenty minutes of footage from the original shoot starring Foster and Capron.

The biggest disappointments in showbiz usually come to those competing in talent shows.

Comedy impressionist Drew Cameron, who had won an episode of Opportunity Knocks in 1969 at the age of twelve, found that performers on Britain's Got Talent have often been 'dumped' after receiving rave reviews from the judges.

Drew made a big impression in every sense when he appeared on BGT in 2008. But he took the good luck message 'break a leg' too literally by fracturing his left leg two weeks later and was unable to return.

Even so, Drew was disappointed with parts of the show's format including the way contestants' hopes of achieving stardom were raised and then dashed. He told me: "BGT present some talented people into the media but the television industry provides no other entertainment shows for them to aspire to."

He added: "I couldn't produce a show in that manner, though I realise that the public do love BGT. Simon Cowell knows what the general public will accept and he has made millions!

"I took part in BGT in the early years when they didn't use professional acts, so I pretended I was an amateur. A camera crew came backstage and asked me how much it was my dream. I was shocked, and told them that I wasn't twelve years of age - it wasn't my dream to win a talent contest!"

Neither did Drew claim he was doing it for his children or his granny!

Looking back, he reflected: "I now understand it is a game you play to get more exposure and money. I didn't play the game."

Drew underlined what a talented performer he is by being voted the Best Variety Act of 2013 at the National Entertainment Awards.

As a former public relations executive, I would like to offer some free advice to Simon Cowell: Stop putting on acts who are so bad the audience laugh at them instead of with them, and try to show the kind, helpful, generous side of your nature more often, especially when giving critical critiques.

Telling a contestant they were "completely and utterly horrific" was no doubt a shattering experience for them. So while Simon's cutting remarks as a judge often prove very funny to the audience, is it worth getting a laugh at the expense of leaving the performer devastated?

I agree Cowell should continue to be critical of poor performances, but there's no need to come out with insults such as "You look like the Incredible Hulk's wife."

If you take my advice on board, Simon, your popularity will increase further - and you'll encourage even more talented people to come on your show!

CHAPTER THIRTY-SIX

Manchester City not as great as Arsenal Invincibles says Supermac

Most football managers deserve the mega bucks they earn because they come in for so much criticism and usually end up getting the sack.

Former players often find it preferable to become pundits, and in most cases are doing a very good job in giving fans the benefit of their expertise and opinions.

I greatly enjoy the views of Alan Shearer, Jermaine Jenas, Gary Neville, Ian Wright, Lee Dixon, Graeme Souness, Jamie Carragher, Martin Keown, Jamie Redknapp and Rio Ferdinand, though, of course, I don't always agree with them.

And when I want a laugh I listen to the error-prone Chris Kamara on Sky's Soccer Saturday reports. His worst bloomer had the whole studio in stitches when he failed to spot a sending off during Portsmouth's draw with Blackburn on April 3rd, 2010.

I know from my days as Sky TV's Controller of Information that watching a TV monitor and a match at the same time can be difficult, but it adds to the likeable Kamara's problems - and his appeal - when he occasionally gets his words jumbled.

Fortunately, presenter Jeff Stelling and fellow reporters Matt Le Tissier, Phil Thompson, Paul Merson and Charlie Nicholas are usually on the ball!

Soccer pundits rarely sit on the fence and after Manchester City's amazing triumph in retaining the title by holding off the formidable challenge of Liverpool last season, the outspoken Shearer declared that they were "the best side we have ever seen in the Premier League."

Shearer, himself one of the greatest strikers in the modern era, said in his Sun column: "Manchester United won the treble and Arsenal's Invincibles went unbeaten - but this City side eclipses the lot. To romp to the title (the previous season) with 100 points and then to back that up with 98 points is extraordinary.

"To get over the line, with Liverpool matching them step for step in such an intense and relentless run-in, sets City apart."

Alan made his claim even before City slammed Watford 6-0 in the FA Cup final to become the first team in English football to win a domestic treble.

But another Newcastle goal-scoring legend, Malcolm Macdonald, thinks Shearer is wrong. Supermac told me: "I disagree with Alan. To me the Arsenal Invincibles are the best Premiership team ever. To go the whole of the 2003–04 season unbeaten in the league is a fantastic achievement that is unmatched. And Arsène Wenger's team played scintillating football."

Macdonald is a former Gunner, of course, but he insists: "Arsenal going the entire season without a single defeat in the league, gaining 26 wins and 12 draws, speaks for itself. I would also rate the Manchester United team that won a treble of Premier League, FA Cup and Champions League in 1998-9 slightly above City. United were so powerful and made winning look easy.

"I saw City lose to Newcastle in January - their fourth league defeat of the season - and they disappointed me. But they then bounced back magnificently to win every remaining league game. I'd like to see a bit more from City and they might well produce it next season, but Liverpool have a great team, too, so we should see another battle royal."

Macdonald[*], a superb centre-forward who scored 204 goals in 421 games, remains a big favourite of mine as both a player and a man.

The shrewd Arsène Wenger deserved great credit for getting his teams to produce such attractive football, and playing to individual strengths. This was the case with another favourite of mine, Ian Wright, who was nearly 33 when Wenger arrived at Highbury in September 1996, but the new boss still got a lot of goals out of him.

I interviewed Wrighty a couple of times during his days at Crystal Palace, where he was their greatest ever striker, and what he said as a player also applies to him as a pundit.

He modestly stated: "I just want to be remembered for being a hardworking, honest professional who did the best he could with the opportunity he got."

Wright certainly made the most of the opportunities football, and more recently, television, have given him after spending two weeks in Chelmsford Prison as a youngster in 1982 for non-payment of driving fines.

Ian's former Arsenal team-mates Keown and Dixon and Liverpool idol Graeme Souness are also equally sharp and astute as pundits as they were as players. And I love listening to Graeme and Co. expertly analyse teams' strengths and weaknesses with the aid of play-backs.

In contrast, the BBC's meagre sports slots on their news programmes are, in my view, usually inadequate. Their short snippets of top football action often fail to show all the goals - and on some occasions they do not even identify the scorers!

What infuriates me most is when the sports presenters on Breakfast use up some of what little time they are given by indulging in chit-chat with the programme's hosts!

If I was their producer I would tell them to opt for more action and less banter.

It is vital to make the most of the time you have on TV and get important messages across. Gareth Southgate, Jermaine Jenas, Peter Crouch, Thierry Henry and Danny Rose did that by appearing with HRH the Duke of Cambridge on BBC's A Royal Team Talk: Tackling Mental Health.

The insightful Jermaine said: "It's often neglected and overlooked, but talking about men's mental health is so important." He then helped sufferers to do so with his sympathetic and understanding approach to their problems.

Malcolm Macdonald provides more interesting views and facts in his book 'Supermac: My Autobiography', published in August, 2004.

CHAPTER THIRTY-SEVEN

Million-to-one shot not repeated at roulette table

Getting a free honeymoon trip to Las Vegas, New Orleans and Hawaii sounds incredible - and so it was! But things didn't work out so well when I tried to uphold my part of the bargain with travel company Kuoni.

While my wife-to-be Heather and I were planning our wedding in 2000 I hit on the idea of arranging our honeymoon as a Press facility trip.

It came about because when I was making one of my regular appearances on BBC News 24 as a sports pundit I noticed the name Jeremy Skidmore on their schedule.

Jeremy had worked for me on the notorious Sunday Sport years earlier and was now editor of a travel magazine, so I felt he should be in a position to commission an article from me.

Tracking him down took longer than I expected, but then I had an amazing stroke of good fortune. I was covering a soccer match between Charlton Athletic and Wolves one Saturday afternoon for The People and rushed into a newsagent's shop near The Valley shortly before kick-off to buy a paper.

There in the shop was the very contact I needed. No, not the travel magazine, nor one of their representatives, but Jeremy Skidmore himself! The chances of that happening were a million to one - even allowing for the fact Jeremy was going to the same match as a devoted Wolves fan.

It convinced me that this was meant to be - and perhaps was a sign I would enjoy the same sort of luck at the gambling tables in Vegas.

Jeremy agreed to me writing a feature for him on the basis that it would have a new slant because Heather and I were older honeymooners in our 50s.

I did an excellent deal with Kuoni that, in exchange for the coverage I would be providing, they'd give me a free tailor-made holiday to the three dream locations of Vegas, New Orleans and Hawaii - and Heather would get a reasonable discount.

Heather and I had a fabulous time, including upgrades to a wonderful suite in our luxury hotel in New Orleans, and so I was able to write a very positive review - too positive as it turned out.

Jeremy explained that I had been too gushing in my praise, and, as the editor of a travel magazine read by the trade, he needed to paint a more balanced picture.

So I re-wrote the article, which was still very complimentary, but now also focused on those holiday features that could have been slightly improved upon.

Jeremy liked the story and asked me to be patient as he felt it would be diplomatic to let his features editor decide when to use it. Unfortunately, within weeks, Jeremy had left the travel magazine, and the features editor chose not to use an article which she had been presented with by her former editor, rather than commissioning herself.

I was left with the unenviable task of explaining the situation to the Press Officer of Kuoni and leaving them to negotiate with the new editor to use the article.

Despite the concessions given to us, including complimentary tickets to top shows, our stay in Las Vegas still cost me a lot of money - in gambling.

When we arrived at the Mirage Hotel, Heather was tired and wanted to have a sleep so I went down to the casino alone to play roulette. Needless to say, I did not enjoy the same good fortune that had brought me into contact with my old mate 'Skidders' back in Charlton.

I tried out my 'system', based on the belief that it was most unlikely the roulette ball would land on the same colour ten times in succession. So, after waiting for four blacks to come up in a row, I started betting on red and tripled my stake every time I lost.

The problem was that the Mirage casino imposed a higher minimum stake on even-money bets than casinos in England - so continually trebling up became expensive.

I soon ran out of dollars and the croupier held up the game while I went across to a booth to get around £300 exchanged in order that I could again triple my bet on the next spin of the wheel. It made no difference and I kept losing - probably £500 in all. Some system, eh?

When I sheepishly returned to our bedroom Heather asked me why I looked rather depressed. I didn't have the heart to tell her the full story and just blurted out that I'd had some bad luck in the casino during the half an hour I'd been away!

Heather eventually got the truth out of me and said: "Never mind, darling. Now I won't feel guilty when I spend lots at the shops!"

Pre-planning is always important, and everything, including the connecting flights, went like clockwork. But Heather was not too impressed with my decision to arrange for an inhabitant of Las Vegas - a friend of a friend in London - to show us around.

Our 'guide' Robert, a larger-than-life Texan, complete with cowboy hat and boots, proved to be an extremely helpful gay guy, who seemed to take rather a shine to me. He insisted I sit in the front of his Cadillac with him on our sight-seeing trips and that I go to a hotel to take part in an organised card game with him while Heather was 'packed off' to the shops. Needless to say, he gave me far more of his attention than he did my lovely bride!

Incidentally, the card session resulted in more losses and taught me that gambling is usually a mug's game.

Ironically, Heather was also 'overlooked' when we went to China and climbed the Great Wall.

It was a sweltering hot day and our Chinese tour guide, aware that a big fellow like me was struggling with the steep slope as we approached the Wall, decided to give me a hand. So he got behind me and pushed me up the cobbled hill.

What he didn't notice - and neither did I - was that Heather, who had been suffering with a virus, was lagging behind and close to fainting!

Our superb holiday to three cities in China and Hong Kong was also with Kuoni and I was pleased to be able to write a very positive review about it.

The only other time I had difficulty in delivering what I had promised to a travel company for a Press facility trip was when I was at Sunday Sport.

I had persuaded the Press Officer at Thomas Cook to give me a free holiday to Hong Kong, Singapore and Bangkok in exchange for a prominent feature story, and this was with the blessing of our unconventional Editor-in-chief Mike Gabbert.

But upon my return, the sometimes eccentric Gabbert told me on Press day that he had a space to fill on a news page and wanted to shove my holiday article in it. When I saw that the space was only two columns wide, in the middle of the page, with no room for a picture, I was horrified.

I told Gabbert that we could not throw a holiday feature story away like this when we had a commitment to the travel company. But Mike, whose stubborn streak had seen him play a key part in The People uncovering the soccer match fixing scandal involving England players Peter Swan and Tony Kay, along with David Layne, in 1964, would not budge. He even used a frivolous headline about how I had bought a cheap suit in Bangkok.

I was horrified - and so was the Press Officer at Thomas Cook. But I retrieved the situation by arranging for a double-page feature to be used the following week, with Thomas Cook offering our readers a £50 discount on bookings for long haul holidays.

Although Gabbert was a great journalist, his insistence on sometimes trivialising stories and putting a sexual slant on them, as he did with a news item about an attractive female racing driver who was trying to take her sport seriously, caused a few ripples in our otherwise excellent relationship.

When he left Sunday Sport to become Editor of the Daily Star in 1987 he would have taken me with him, but the Star were based in Manchester and I had a commitment, as a divorced parent, to look after my son James, who lived with me near London.

It was just as well I did not go with Mike. Some of the existing Daily Star staff were opposed to their new editor from Sunday Sport, who had been foisted upon them, and this became immediately obvious when Gabbert gave his first editorial briefing.

Apparently, one of the senior female staffers told him in front of her colleagues that if he expected her to 'make up' readers' letters, as she reckoned he had done at Sunday Sport, then he would be greatly disappointed. Not to be outdone, Mike said in a loud stage whisper to one of his assistants "Find me someone who will."

I urged him not to take the Star too far down-market, but he insisted on packing it with girlie pictures and sex-orientated stories.

Advertising and circulation nosedived and within months Gabbert was sacked.

CHAPTER THIRTY-EIGHT

Hanky-panky in the office was cut short

As a teenage reporter I once used the office for some 'hanky-panky' which back-fired on me badly and ended in embarrassment.

I had taken a young lady to the cinema one evening and afterwards we called in the office of my then paper the Kentish Times in Bromley to make a phone call.

One thing led to another and, after some passionate kisses, I cleared one of the editorial desks so that this delightful girl and I could get a little bit more physical. If I remember rightly, it was not long before an item of clothing was loosened.

But, obviously unbeknown to me, John, our chief reporter at that time, couldn't sleep because he feared he had left the office fire on.

So he told his wife he was getting out of bed and returning to his office. John simply put on a coat over his pyjamas, jumped in his car and drove to the Bromley and Kentish Times car park.

He strode into the editorial room just as the young lady and I were getting rather intimate. When she saw another man arriving (and in his pyjamas) she got the wrong impression. The result was that she quickly adjusted her clothing and fled!

But those were great days. I was editing the sports pages and covering the matches of the local amateur football club Bromley.

They had a very forceful chairman called Charlie King, with whom I had a few run-ins. I remember covering one of their games at Clapton where they started with a depleted side because two of their players arrived at the ground after the kick-off.

I saw it as a very good story and went into the dressing room afterwards to interview the two late arrivals. King followed me in and was so furious, because he felt the story would paint the club in a bad light, that he tore up my notebook!

It was due to these sort of exchanges that an actor played me, years later, in the comedy film The Bromley Boys.

Those days prepared me well for later dealing with big name chairmen Ron Noades at Crystal Palace and Brentford, Martin Edwards at Manchester United and Ken Bates at Chelsea. None of them made me as apprehensive as the formidable Charlie King.

I learned not to be intimidated by anyone, no matter how famous or overbearing they might be and how big the occasion was.

My first wife Stephanie and I were not party animals, but we became used to attending all sorts of dinners, dances and functions.

As I got older I mingled more with celebrities, but my second wife Heather was at first frightened about the prospect of meeting them.

I found this out while I was courting her when I took her to a dinner in honour of George Best at the Savoy Hotel in The Strand.

Heather and I were supposed to meet in the Savoy's reception area, but she was so apprehensive about the possibility of bumping into some of the star-studded guests that she waited for me outside the hotel. Fortunately, when we later talked to Michael Parkinson and his wife Mary, they immediately put her at ease with their friendly manner.

CHAPTER THIRTY-NINE

Even the cast criticised Durbridge play

Chatting with celebrities can be fun - the trick is knowing what questions to ask them if you want to find out anything meaningful!

Anyone can mingle with big name actors by going to first nights of London productions - I found myself chatting to Roger Lloyd Pack, Arlene Phillips, Kate Thornton and Holly Willoughby in the bar at one production alone - or joining a 'friends group' at your local theatre.

In Eastbourne, the normal custom of The Friends of the Devonshire Park Theatre has been to invite the cast to have drinks with members in the bar after the first night performance.

This has resulted in myself and other members having enjoyable chats with the likes of Susan Penhaligon, Joanne Heywood, Joanna Van Gyseghem, Liza Goddard, former Dr Who Colin Baker, Susie Amy, Jennifer Bryden, Denis Lill, former pop star-turned-actor Mark Wynter, Neil Roberts and my now good friend Brian Capron.

During these get-togethers you can find out some interesting titbits of information. For example, Mark

Wynter, who I had first met, together with fellow singer Helen Shapiro, when they were in the hit parade back in the 1960s, shared some amusing backstage stories with me, while Neil Roberts told me how his son Thomas had written a cookery book with a difference called 'Meals In The Limelight' containing recipes from celebrities. It tells you about what Arnold Schwarzenegger has for breakfast, Keira Knightley's favourite cake and Judi Dench's ideal dessert.

Of course, when meeting celebrities it is easy to say the wrong thing and perhaps dent their egos. I forgot that Roger Lloyd-Pack, best known for his TV roles in 'Only Fools And Horses' and 'The Vicar of Dibley', had been in the film 'Harry Potter and the Goblet of Fire' and referred to a completely different film. But like, Susie Amy, who I mistakenly called by her surname, he let me off with an indulgent smile.

Colin Baker meets members of The Friends of Devonshire Park Theatre

The same applied with Colin Baker, who was playing the role of Inspector Morse in 'House of Ghosts' when I met him. He picked me up on a malapropism, but said he had a forgiving nature, as he seemed to prove previously by touring with his ex-wife Liza Goddard in 'She Stoops To Conquer' in 2008.

Some touring productions include several well-known actors, as was the case with 'Fatal Encounter' by Francis Durbridge, which came to Devonshire Park Theatre in September 2009.

A big smile from Anita Harris

It starred Nicholas Ball ('EastEnders' and 'Hazell'), singer-actress Anita Harris and Neil Stacy ('Duty Free'), a very talented trio who were a delight to meet. Unfortunately, it was not one of Durbridge's best thrillers - and even cast members admitted it lacked credibility. My review in the Brighton Argus was actually kinder than the opinions some of the actors expressed!

Former Friends chairman Harry Lederman, sadly no longer with us, introduced me to celebrities at other functions, including a very pleasant Kevin Pallister, the star of West End musical 'Blood Brothers'.

It was Harry who arranged for the film premiere of my comedy 'Hacking It' to be shown at the Winter Garden Theatre, Eastbourne, after he and fellow movie maker Alan Tutt had filmed it. Executive director Alan G. Baker has since sent it to television companies as a suggested pilot for a sitcom so some day you may even get the chance to view it.

If you want to see the DVD, starring Dean Matthews, Mandy Lloyd and other actors from Seaford Little Theatre, get in touch with me at tflood04@yahoo.co.uk. It is a real hoot!

Hopefully 'Hacking It' will enjoy more screen time than my wife Heather was given as an extra in the film Brighton Rock - blink and you'll miss her!

Since Heather and I became authors, we have made ourselves available to give talks and do book readings and signings.

My biggest piece of advice to would-be authors is: be ruthless in rewriting your work and be persistent with approaches to publishers. Remember that J.K. Rowling was rejected many times by publishers before getting her first Harry Potter book accepted - so don't give up.

Make sure you start with a very interesting first paragraph that will immediately 'hook' readers. If you are writing an autobiography, do not begin with your birth, but start with one of the biggest - or most amusing - moments of your life.

You can help yourself greatly by getting others to read your manuscript and provide advice. Then be prepared to amend it further, and, when you are finally satisfied, offer it to more than one agent or publisher (after finding out first that they accept unsolicited manuscripts).

Landing a publishing deal is only the beginning for an author! These days they are expected to carry out a lot of their own marketing, including arranging book signings, readings and talks and requesting support from friends on Facebook etc!

It is also important for authors to seek out celebrities or 'experts' in the subject they have written about, and ask them to endorse their books, as Heather and I have done.

As I mentioned previously, my fantasy adventure 'The Secret Potion' was recommended by late actress June Whitfield as an ideal follow up to Harry Potter, while Heather's books for younger children, 'Mousey Mousey and the Witches' Spells' and 'Giant Sticker Monster and Other Children's Stories', have been compared favourably by reviewers to Beatrix Potter and Enid Blyton. Her fantasy adventure Purple Mist has been described by author and poet Laurie Wilkinson as "a rollercoaster of thrills, spills and fun which children from six to 15 should love".

My own spicy crime thriller Triple Tease has been endorsed by best-selling authors Peter James and Tamara McKinley, actors Brian Capron and Alan Baker, director Patric Kearns and the Sun newspaper's Stuart Pink.

Authors can also approach their local Member of Parliament or Mayor to launch or endorse their books. Eastbourne MP Stephen Lloyd and Mayors Carolyn Heaps and Gill Mattock have made warm tributes to our books.

Always be on the lookout for marketing opportunities and join as many writing groups as possible, such as Anderida Writers - or form one yourself as children's author Diny van Kleeff has done with Authors of Eastbourne. It is well worth looking up Diny's own books on her Facebook page, and if you would like to obtain signed copies of books by Heather and myself at discounted prices, go to:

www.fantasyadventurebooks.com and
www.celebritiesconfessions.com

You can also check us out on three videos on You Tube which should make you laugh. Hopefully, this book has also brought a few smiles to your faces.

Oh, and I've not even mentioned my brush with royalty, have I?

They don't come much more famous than the lady with the corgis, do they?

I met her in 2011, and I'm the only one to have been cheeky enough to say to her: "Your majesty, how long have you been impersonating Jeannette Charles?"

But it was look-alike Jeannette Charles, dressed as the Queen, to whom I was speaking - NOT the Queen herself!

Jeannette had a great sense of humour and gave me a ticking off, telling me: "You are a most disrespectful subject."

CHAPTER FORTY

Charlton's 'Di Stéfano'

So who are my all-time favourite sports heroes?

Of the current stars I would pick football wizards Cristiano Ronaldo and Lionel Messi.

But my No.1 former sports hero will greatly surprise you. George Best and Muhammad Ali would be second and third, but my absolute favourite was someone many people will not even have heard of.

He was Stuart Leary, a footballer with Charlton Athletic, the team I followed as a boy, and a cricketer with Kent.

Leary was a deep lying centre-forward in the mould of Real Madrid legend Alfredo Di Stéfano. He was a prolific marksman and became Charlton's all-time record league scorer with 153 goals from 1951 to 1962. But it was his great vision and inch-perfect passing that made him so outstanding.

For many years Stuart, a South African, managed to fit in his summer job of playing cricket for Kent with his football career. But when Frank Hill became Charlton manager he didn't like the fact that Leary would start pre-season football training late while completing the cricket season.

A battle of wills resulted. It seemed Charlton would do the unthinkable and part with their star player due mainly to what many fans perceived as their manager's stubbornness.

Stuart went home to South Africa and the English Press could not contact him. So I posted a letter to him, containing a list of questions about the situation, and he sent me back a full and frank reply.

I sold the story to the national Press and, for good measure, added that the words 'Hill must go' were daubed on the wall outside the Charlton ground.

I had let my feelings as a devoted supporter conflict with my journalist judgement. But to ensure my story was true, I went down to The Valley at the dead of night, found a suitable wall and wrote the offending words on it.

It almost broke my heart - and Leary's - when in 1962 Stuart eventually moved to QPR where he never quite showed the same level of brilliance he had consistently displayed at Charlton.

Despite being South African born, Leary had appeared in the England Under 23 team, but the Football Association banned non-English-born players from representing the seniors.

Stuart was not just a great player, he was also a wonderful bloke. So it was a tragedy when he died in controversial circumstances at the age of 55.

His body was discovered dead on Table Mountain in South Africa on August 23, 1988 - four days after his car had been found abandoned.

Charlton have one claim to fame that even the likes of Manchester United and Chelsea cannot match - they produced the greatest comeback in football history by amazingly rallying from 5-1 down to beat Huddersfield 7-6 with 10 men in the old Division Two at The Valley in 1957.

Only 12,535 people saw this incredible match and I was not among them - it was one of the few home matches I missed that season as a devoted 14-year-old fan.

Charlton had lost centre-half and skipper Derek Ufton, who was carried off with a dislocated shoulder in the 17th minute, and nobody gave them a chance when they trailed 5-1 to Bill Shankly's Huddersfield with 28 minutes remaining.

But, with the immaculate Leary pulling the strings, and Johnny Summers, a journeyman left-winger, playing the game of his life to score five goals after changing his disintegrating boots, Charlton went 6-5 ahead.

Four minutes from the end Huddersfield drew level at 6-6 when a shot from Stan Howard was deflected into his own net by John Hewie, and it seemed the Robins would be denied a sensational win.

But in the dying seconds Summers crossed for John 'Buck' Ryan to score his second goal of the game and give Charlton an unbelievable victory.

Tragically, the Robins' hero Summers died of cancer within five years of his epic performance.

During my time as a sports writer I had a couple of run-ins with former Charlton manager Alan Curbishley because of my criticisms of his striker Carl Leaburn's lack of goals.

Leaburn became a cult figure as a striker who rarely scored - his record was a meagre 57 goals in 389 league appearances with Charlton, Northampton, MK Dons and QPR from 1987 to 2002 (just 0.14 a game)!

A hard-hitting match report I wrote for Sunday paper The People particularly upset Curbishley. He took the opportunity to criticise what I had said, while defending Leaburn and his own team selection, in an article in the local Charlton newspaper the South East London Mercury.

What Curbishley did not seem to consider was that the Mercury might offer me the right of reply. They actually invited me to give my views and used them as the back page lead story the following week.

The main point I made was that Leaburn might be a good target man, but his goals record was so poor he failed to reach double figures most seasons, which meant his strike partner would probably need to score at least 30 a season to make Charlton a successful side. This was simply not practical. I don't think Curbishley was best pleased, but hopefully he accepted that I felt as strongly about the matter as he did!

CHAPTER FORTY-ONE

How I was deceived into writing a lie

THE first story I ever had published turned out to be a lie!

It was back in the early 1960s and I had just landed my first job as a junior reporter on the Lewisham Borough News, but still had a few weeks to go before completing my education at the South East London Day College, which was also in Lewisham.

A party of students from the college went on a day trip (to Oxford, if I remember correctly). Two of the boys in our group took a punt out on the river and came back soaking wet from head to foot.

They told us how a small girl had fallen into the river and they had dived in to save her. So I wrote a story for the Borough News about local boys rescuing drowning girl and they printed it on their front page.

Only then did the two boys reveal they had made up the tale about the girl in the river. They confessed to me that they were fooling around on a punt and fell in, but were so scared of the master in charge that they invented a story about them being heroes!

My early days as a journalist were spent covering Greenwich court, flower shows, community meetings and the like. My most 'exciting' story at that time was the revelation at a rather boring meeting that some coal merchants doused their sacks in water to make them heavier!

But the Borough News Sports Editor John Richards gave me the chance to report on Charlton, Crystal Palace and Millwall. When he left I took over his job and, at 19, was probably the youngest sports editor in the country.

My career path took me to the Kentish Times Series, the Slough Observer Series, the Sunday Express as a parttimer, the Lancashire Evening Telegraph and Star, Football Monthly, Sunday Sport, Fleet Street News Agency, Sky Television, the Richmond and Twickenham Times Series, the News of the World and The People.

Tony dishes out awards with help from Trevor Brooking (left) and David Lloyd

I still keep my hand in as Managing Director of agency Sportsworld Communications, but I have retired from full time journalism and now spend most of my time as an author and theatre critic.

As I said earlier, the most emotive story I have ever written was my exclusive interview with Liverpool goalkeeper Bruce Grobbelaar the day after he played for Liverpool against Nottingham Forest in the Hillsborough Disaster which killed 96 people at Sheffield Wednesday's football ground on April 15, 1989.

I did not report on Liverpool matches, but obtained other exclusive interviews with some of their players and former manager Bob Paisley.

My interview with Paisley came soon after I left Sunday Sport, together with the two full-time members of my staff, in protest at the paper's weird news stories having an adverse effect on our sports coverage.

The three of us had been phoning around Fleet Street asking if there were any suitable jobs, and this included a conversation with the Sports Editor of The Sun, who had no vacancies.

Immediately afterwards I landed a job as Sports Editor of Fleet Street News Agency where my main task was to set up a new sports section, producing and marketing stories to national papers in competition with vastly larger agencies such as the Press Association and Exchange Telegraph.

What I needed was a big exclusive to get us off to a good start. So I contacted Paisley, who in 1983 had completed nine glorious years as Liverpool manager during which he led them to six League titles, three European Cups, one UEFA Cup, three League Cups, five Community Shields and a UEFA Super Club.

The man regarded by many as the greatest Liverpool manager of all time did not usually give in-depth interviews, but he made an exception with me. I suggested that he hit back at criticisms of the club and himself, and I gleefully contacted every Fleet Street sports editor to offer them the story.

They all took my calls with the exception of the Sun's Sports Editor. Perhaps he thought I was still trying to persuade him to give me a job, but the upshot was that I gave the story to everyone apart from him. The next morning it made headlines almost everywhere, and The Sun felt obliged to run a follow-up story a day later.

Interviews with England bosses Bobby Robson, Howard Wilkinson and Terry Venables, and Brian Barwick when he first took over as the FA chief executive in 2005, brought me further big exclusives.

But I berated Venables for not giving his most talented mid-field player Matt Le Tissier a run in the England team.

While chatting to Venables on the phone during his England reign from 1994 to 1996 I told him I felt he had discarded Le Tissier without giving him a real chance to prove himself.

El Tel said he had some sympathy with my view, but he picked teams he felt were most likely to get results.

So flair player Le Tiss was sacrificed. It was criminal that the man hailed as 'Le God' by his adoring Southampton fans gained only eight England caps.

Competing against the whole of Fleet Street wasn't easy because national newspapers, television and other agencies had far more staff, better resources and, in many cases, more contacts. But I obtained a fair share of column inches.

I made endless telephone calls to achieve other headline-making interviews with managers such as Arsenal's George Graham, Manchester United's Alex Ferguson, Charlton's Lennie Lawrence, Steve Gritt and Alan Curbishley and Spurs' Terry Venables and Peter Shreeve. Others who gave me their time and assistance with stories included Don Howe, David Pleat, Steve Coppell, Brentford's opinionated managers Martin Allen and Terry Butcher, former Liverpool star Tommy Smith, and, of course, Tommy Docherty.

Tony with Terry Butcher

Questioning football club chairmen also brought me some great stories, especially Ron Noades during the time he was being hounded by fans at Brentford over spending costs and the threat of losing their beloved Griffin Park ground.

My relationship with Ken Bates while he was at Chelsea was rather different. He gave me more cash than quotes!

Ken was very interested in Britain's oldest football magazine Football Monthly where I was editor and co-owner.

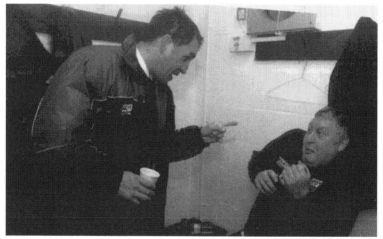

Martin Allen demands more from this under-performing player

We got talking about the fact that the magazine was having financial difficulties, and the result was Bates actually bought Football Monthly from me and my partner Peter Rea. He kept us on as consultants and treated us very fairly, even extending my contract. So presumably he thought our ideas had some merit because Ken doesn't suffer fools lightly!

CHAPTER FORTY-TWO

James Cracknell's life-risking ordeals

Few British sportsmen have had as many ups and downs as double Olympic gold medallist rower James Cracknell.

His latest high was becoming the oldest winner of the university Boat Race, with Cambridge, at the age of 45 this year.

James' worst low was suffering a horrific brain injury after a road accident in 2010 which changed his relationship with his wife, sports presenter Beverley Turner, and eventually led to them separating.

I met Cracknell some years ago when he told me how he had risked his life in the pursuit of glory.

He said that winning gold medals at the Sydney 2000 and Athens 2004 Olympics were a walk in the park compared with conquering the Atlantic in the world's toughest rowing race.

Cracknell revealed: "Driving myself to near exhaustion in the Atlantic Rowing Race with Ben Fogle in 2005 after 2,930 miles and 49 days, in which we encountered the worst weather in the history of the event, was a living hell at times.

"We could have lost our lives when the boat was capsized by a giant wave. We wept, fought, played games, grew beards, nursed blisters and sat on agonisingly sore bottoms, but somehow kept rowing.

"It was harder and in many respects a bigger achievement than my double Olympic gold medals, my three world records or my six world titles."

Although Cracknell and Fogle were the first pair home (overall, they were third to finish behind two men's fours), the use of ballast water during the race resulted in them being moved to second position in the pairs.

CHAPTER FORTY-THREE

Journalists' lives can be very stressful

Working as a journalist certainly wasn't as gruelling as rowing almost 3,000 miles, like James Cracknell did, but it was, nevertheless, a stressful, demanding, very competitive job, requiring me to put in ridiculously long hours.

It makes life difficult for you and your partner and family.

Fortunately, I had benefited from a great home life as a youngster thanks to my loving grandparents Reg and Winifred Burwash, who brought me up, and my mother Mabel, who was always there for me despite having to cope with poor health and her two divorces. These three wonderful people did so much for me. Their love and kindness provided me with a positive outlook and a feeling of security that helped me cope with life's many problems.

Coming from a broken family had some tearful downsides, but visits to my father Dennis and my other grandparents Wal and Rose were happy occasions. And my stepfather George was also kind to me.

I later enjoyed the full support of my first wife Stephanie until our marriage - which had given me happiness and three children - eventually failed.

In more recent years I have been lucky enough to receive the marvellous backing of my second wife Heather, a gorgeous lady with a smile as big as her heart.

Heather and I celebrate a wedding anniversary

One of the happiest days of my life was when I married Heather in Richmond in 2002, with her son Lee giving her away, my son James being best man and our daughters Joanne and Emma bridesmaids.

My speech got plenty of chuckles, but I was upstaged by the normally shy James, whose ribbing of me and my faults had his sisters Joanne and Tracey and others in fits of laughter.

The roles were reversed when I gave a speech as joint best man at James's wedding to his charming bride Gosia in Poland. Cracking jokes that needed to be translated from English to Polish was difficult, but James's friends filled me with confidence by giving me a cheer before I even uttered a word.

I have also benefited from the friendships of first, second and third cousins and relatives through marriages in the Flood, Burwash, Newson, Greatorex and Curtis families. They come from far and wide, with the Newsons playing a big part in the history of Felixstowe Ferry.

One of the happiest days of Tony's life

CHAPTER FORTY-FOUR

Authors and characters I love

Intriguing plots are obviously important in books of fiction, but great characters are also essential - and they can have a big influence on readers.

Some fictional characters come out with gems of advice such as the lovable Mr Micawber in Charles Dicken's David Copperfield. His recipe for happiness was: "Annual income twenty pounds, annual expenditure nineteen [pounds], nineteen [shillings] and six [pence], result happiness. Annual income twenty pounds, annual expenditure twenty pounds, nought and six, result misery."

Books combining fact with fiction can help to educate and inspire youngsters. For example, the rags to riches story of Dick Whittington and his cat is not just a fairy-tale. The real Dick Whittington was Lord Mayor of London in 1397, 1406 and 1419.

Modern authors I greatly enjoy are Jeffrey Archer - particularly his excellent can't-put-down tales 'Not A Penny More, Not A Penny Less', 'Shall We Tell The President' and 'A Prisoner of Birth' - and Peter James, especially his equally enthralling thrillers featuring Brighton-based Detective Superintendent Roy Grace. Peter's stories are so good that some of them have been successfully staged as sell-out plays.

I can also recommend Simon Kernick's thriller 'Relentless' and most of Lee Child's Jack Reacher series, although I was disappointed in 'Night School'.

You may also like to check out my own spicy thriller 'Triple Tease' and my fantasy adventure 'Secret Potion'. I did a lot of research on police procedures for Triple Tease as it is so important to get them right.

They should be spot on in books written by former coppers such as T.J. Walter, whose crime thrillers include 'The Body in the River'.

I love autobiographies, especially those written by many of the showbiz and sports stars I have spoken about in earlier chapters.

One piece of advice I would give to potential readers when selecting a book is to look carefully at some of the endorsements and reviews. If praise is given to the author rather than the book then it could mean that the reviewer has not actually read it!

To discover more about books and entertainment, visit my website page:

www.facebook.com/EXCHANGINGTIPS

where you can also give your views and spread the word about your own books or projects.

CHAPTER FORTY-FIVE

Jonah Lomu and Debbie McGee have been inspirations

Finally, let me urge you all to look on the bright side by referring you to the example set by one of the biggest sporting heroes I ever met, the late rugby super star Jonah Lomu.

The giant Newlander, who, at 19st 10lb and 6ft 5in, towered over me, won 63 caps as an All Black and was the Rugby World Cup all-time top try scorer with 15 tries before being struck down by illness.

Lomu was diagnosed with nephrotic syndrome, a serious kidney disorder, in 1995.

By 2003 he was on dialysis and in 2004 underwent a kidney transplant.

Jonah later attempted a comeback, but did not play international rugby again, and retired from the professional game in 2007. He died, aged just 40, on November 18th, 2015 after suffering a heart attack associated with his kidney condition.

He was so positive when I met him before his illness and he remained so while trying to make a comeback after it.

Lomu said: "I had been running straight over people, scoring tries, winning games and having fun. Then I ended up so sick that I couldn't even run past a little baby. So I'm just glad to be able to enjoy life again and do what I love most."

Unfortunately, his recovery didn't last long, but Jonah Lomu's inspirational message was that we should be thankful for what we've got!

Jonah Lomu bends down to fit in the picture

Coping with adversity is very difficult. One example has been set by TV star Debbie McGee.

I briefly met Debbie when she appeared with her late husband, magician Paul Daniels, as his assistant, at the Royal Hippodrome Theatre, Eastbourne, back in November 2013.

Debbie was devastated when Paul died three years later, but she bravely battled on. She competed in Strictly Come Dancing in 2017 and was an extremely popular finalist. Then, in March 2018, she took part in a 15-day, 26km trek across France and Spain with other celebs.

Debbie again showed great courage when, later that year, she was diagnosed with early-stage breast cancer and had surgery to remove two tumours.

My wife Heather underwent surgery to have part of a lung removed in April, 2019 so we know how stressful that can be.

Singer-actress Anita Harris, still working at 77, also found life difficult after suffering a financial crisis.

She and husband Mike Margolis lost £1million following a Swiss bank collapse in 1985.

The couple twice had to give up their homes to help pay off debts.

But Anita told me: "Mike and I remain thankful for the good things life has given us. We count our blessings all the time."

Heather and I fully endorse this sentiment. Having a sense of humour is also important, and we have managed to make each other laugh virtually every day since we've been together.

ENDORSEMENTS FOR THE FIRST EDITION

The late actress JUNE WHITFIELD had this to say about the first edition:

"As a former Fleet Street journalist and Sky Television executive, Tony Flood has been able to put together a host of revealing anecdotes and interviews involving big name celebrities in My Life With The Stars.

Sports fans and show business followers will enjoy reading about star names ranging from Muhammad Ali, Bobby Moore and George Best to Frank Sinatra, The Beatles and Bruce Forsyth. So happy page turning!"

***

If you want to know the ins and outs of show biz, sport, films and politics this is the one!

Tony Flood takes us on a riotous trip through the years of chatting with and writing about so many of the great names...George Best, Muhammad Ali, Eric Morecame, Bruce Forsyth, Kylie Minogue etc.

Tony has all the latest shenanigans as well as the ancient stuff ...the kids will love it and so will the old timers.

I just love a good yarn and Tony's book is full of them, including my Beatles story. There is something magical in hearing the frailties of the huge names ...Sir Ralph Richardson forgetting his lines! - **DEC CLUSKEY, THE BACHELORS.**

I much enjoyed reading the many anecdotes in Tony Flood's book, and those people with a love of show business or sport should find this a great read. I am very happy to endorse My Life With the Stars. **- SHIRLEY ANNE FIELD, actress.**

***

My Life With The Stars is full of cheeky anecdotes, and is perfect for fans of entertainment, sport and of those who play it. This interesting book is packed with stories from Tony's life, and the diverse and fascinating people who he has met along the way. I love reading about George Best, a man that I, too, was lucky enough to meet. **- SUSIE AMY, actress.**

***

Tony Flood's dealings with Muhammad Ali, George Best, Bobby Moore and Kenny Dalglish, plus a host of showbiz celebrities, make fascinating reading. WOW! So many of the stars' secrets come out!

The most gripping interview was Tony's exclusive with former Liverpool goalkeeper Bruce Grobelaar the day after the Hillsborough disaster, the deadliest stadium-related tragedy in British history. Revealing how Grobelaar tried to help dying fans while the match was still being played was a remarkable story. **- SAMI MOKBEL, Daily Mail sports writer.**

Retired tabloid journalist Tony Flood has compiled a wonderful list of anecdotes, featuring a galaxy of stars from the worlds of sport, entertainment and politics. There's Bill Clinton's none-too-subtle chat-up lines, Carly Simon's inadvertent public spanking and George Best's horde of female followers. Tales, too, of theatrical Knights Richardson, Geilgud and my own hero, Olivier. My former 'Murder on the Nile' co-star, the late Kate O'Mara, also provided Tony with a revealing story about Joan Collins. Quite a read! - **DENIS LILL, actor**.

YOUR VIEWS ARE IMPORTANT

Hopefully you will find time to review this book on Amazon, Goodreads or other websites. You can contact me on my books and entertainment Facebook page at:

www.facebook.com/EXCHANGINGTIPS

or via websites:

www.celebritiesconfessions.com

www.fantasyadventurebooks.com

45504900R00139

Printed in Poland
by Amazon Fulfillment
Poland Sp. z o.o., Wrocław